THE WORLD OF GOLDENEYE

A COMPREHENSIVE STUDY
ON THE SEVENTEENTH
JAMES BOND FILM
AND ITS LEGACY

NICOLÁS SUSZCZYK

Copyright © 2019 Nicolás Suszczyk

All rights reserved. No part of this book may be reproduced or utilised in any form or by any means, electronic or mechanical, including photocopying, recording or by any information storage and retrieval system, without permission in writing from the author.

Cover artwork design © Nicolás Suszczyk

goldeneyedossier.blogspot.com

This book is an unofficial work and the author is not associated with MGM or EON Productions. All consulted bibliography is cited except for personal interviews held by the author and dialogues from the 1995 film.

The views and opinions expressed within the interviews on this book are those of the interviewees and do not necessarily reflect the views or opinions of the author.

COPYRIGHT NOTICE:

GoldenEye © 1995 Danjaq Inc. and United Artists Pictures Inc.

GoldenEye © Glidrose Publications Ltd as Trustee. 1995.

GoldenEye: Rogue Agent © 2004 EA Games.

GoldenEye 007 ©1997 Eon Productions & Mac B, Inc. Game copyright Nintendo/Rare

GoldenEye 007 © 2010 Activision.

GoldenEye 007: Reloaded © 2011 Activision.

*In Loving Memory of
Alejandro Suszczyk (1958-2016)
My father, and the real author of this book.*

*Also for my late grandparents,
Juan Suszczyk and María Olga Lesiw,
always keeping an eye on me from up in the sky.*

GET THE UPDATED AND ILLUSTRATED EDITION

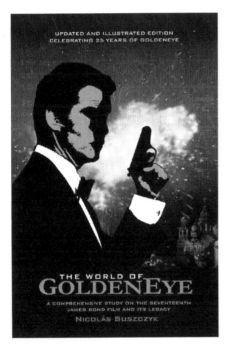

373 PAGES
225 more than the first edition.

ADDITIONAL AND EXPANDED CHAPTERS
GoldenEye and Technology
GoldenEye and Religion

IMAGE GALLERY
with exclusive 'GoldenEye 25' PC mod content

ENCYCLOPAEDIA
with more than 750 entries on GoldenEye, from Ian Fleming's WW2 operation to PC mods.

ONLY AVAILABLE IN PAPERBACK
bit.do/goldeneyeworld

CONTENTS

A WORD FROM THE AUTHOR 7
ABOUT THE BOOK 13
GOLDENEYE AND IAN FLEMING 18
GOLDENEYE AND JAMES BOND 25
GOLDENEYE AND THE COLD WAR 39
GOLDENEYE AND THE FEMALE AUTHORITY 53
GOLDENEYE AND BETRAYAL 65
GOLDENEYE AND ITS GENERATION 75
GOLDENEYE AND FILMMAKING 91
GOLDENEYE AND THE VIDEO GAMES 111
THE LEGACY OF GOLDENEYE 127
GOLDENEYE FACT SHEET 132
GOLDENEYE TIMELINE 134
BIBLIOGRAPHY 140
NOTES 144

A WORD FROM THE AUTHOR

It must have been around December 1997 when I had my first contact with *GoldenEye*, which subsequently led to my passion for James Bond. I was seven years old by then and it was during the summer holiday season in my native Buenos Aires where one day, walking down the street with my father, I saw a street advertisement of Pierce Brosnan holding his Walther PPK handgun, wearing his black tuxedo. It was the announcement for the TV premiere of the film in a very popular Latin American movie channel, Cinecanal, which was due to premiere soon.

For a reason, that image had an impact on me. I have seen action heroes holding their guns in many posters, and I'm quite sure to have seen a man in a dinner jacket before. But the combination of those two in the same person has got my attention for a long while, and then it got familiar: there was a video game for Nintendo 64 which everyone was talking about where that man "with the bow tie" was featured. Of course, I'm from the generation of guys who considered the Nintendo 64 their most coveted prize and I was fascinated with *Super Mario 64*, the launch title of the console. Days later, I went to a toy store where a couple of kids and the shop assistants were playing *GoldenEye*. "What game is that?" I asked. "Oh, the agent 007 one", a kid (probably older than me, maybe even a teen) replied.

I later asked my dad who agent 007, James Bond, was. I can't precisely remember the explanation he gave me, but I was very interested and I urged him to watch that *GoldenEye* movie that inspired the game, as I remembered it was due to get a TV release soon. My dad had seen it before, on the first showing, so he gave me a couple of details. I could hardly wait! So, on January 31, 1998, at 2.40pm, my parents sat with me to watch the film on TV. I was completely riveted! The gun barrel sequence, the action-packed introduction, the main titles with women dancing over communist statues and floating guns (that I must have drawn quite a lot on school notebooks), the tank chase through St. Petersburg, and the antenna climax. Naturally, I also developed an instant crush on Famke Janssen.

It was only a matter of time before dad and I began renting the Nintendo 64 with the game to play after school, and that we watched *Tomorrow Never Dies* and *The World Is Not Enough* on the big screen. Of course, he also initiated me into the older Bonds, primarily Roger Moore, whom he watched on the big screen as a teen. *The Man With The Golden Gun*, *Live And Let Die* and *Moonraker* –in that order– were the first I wanted to see, knowing that the *GoldenEye* game referenced them somehow with the Golden Gun as an available weapon and Jaws and Baron Samedi added to bonus levels. However, *GoldenEye* has always been my number one preference just like Pierce Brosnan is my favourite James Bond.

Flash forward to 2019, I'm an avid James Bond fan. In 2011 I created *The GoldenEye Dossier*, a well-deserved tribute to my favourite films and its video game versions, which is getting a massive update in 2020. You can visit it at goldeneyedossier.blogspot.com, by the way. I have also expressed my love to the seventeenth Bond film in fan sites like *MI6-HQ* (www.mi6-hq.com), *The Spy Command* (hmssweblog.wordpress.com) and *From Sweden with Love* (www.jamesbond007.se), just like I did for *MI6 Confidential* and *Le Bond* magazines in 2015, to celebrate the film's 20th anniversary.

So, what else could I do for the *GoldenEye*'s silver anniversary? Well, I decided to write a book. A book that would explain the huge influence *GoldenEye* had within the Bond franchise and the impact on our generation. To show that it is much more than just a James Bond film and that its quality is many times overlooked. Also, after owning so many *GoldenEye* collectables, why not creating one of my own which I myself could collect and offer you to collect. If I'm not mistaken, the only book exclusively dedicated to the film before mine was the officially licenced *The Making of GoldenEye* by Garth Pearce, which has helped me a lot for the research for this project.

It may feel a bit ridiculous to clarify this, but I feel the need to point this out: English is *not* my mother tongue, even when I speak the language quite well. So, I'm basically thinking in Spanish and writing in English. This text is being periodically revised and amended for possible mistakes or things that didn't sound right for a native speaker. In case there is a small slip-up, I'll humbly apologize and promise to correct those mistakes in future editions.

Before leaving you to enjoy the book, I would like to dedicate it to the memory of my father, who sadly passed away in 2016. If he hadn't told me who James Bond was back then, this book would have probably never existed. I would also thank to my mother, who has always supported my love for this film and franchise, my "brother from another mother" Jack Walter Christian, who has encouraged me to go ahead with this project, and of course to everyone who has grown up adoring this wonderful flick like my pal Yannick Zenhäusern, who has taken his adoration for this film to a huge new level with his fantastic tribute music. There are so many people I would have to thank that a single paragraph wouldn't be enough: Marcos Kontze from *James Bond Brasil*, who has supported my sites and articles from day one, James Page from *MI6-HQ* who has published many of my articles on the world's biggest unofficial Bond site, and Anders Frejdh, the man behind the very popular James Bond site *From Sweden with Love*. A special mention should also deserve my great friend, Adrián Escudero Tanús – thanks to him I now own that advertisement I first saw on the street being a kid!

Thank you to Margarida Araya for giving me many words of advice on this project and some recommendations that were very useful indeed, leading me where to start when the crazy idea of writing a book crossed my mind. Please check out her book: *Timothy Dalton: A Complete Guide to His Film, Television, Stage and Voice Work*. I also thank the collaboration from Matt Spaiser for his help on the details of the James Bond suits and also to Brian McKaig, who reminded me of some connections between *GoldenEye* and the John Gardner novel, *The Man From Barbarossa*.

Also, a special mention deserves a (redundancy intended) special woman. She probably won't like me to name her and I'll respect that, but I have to say that watching *SPECTRE* with her was bigger than any premiere or event in the world. She has also been extremely supportive of my passion and thanks to her I got *GoldenEye* in yet another home video format. So, this book goes especially for you, little lady.

Of course, I don't want to forget thanking God for giving me the opportunity to write this book: the expertise, the technology, the tools of the trade and the chance to bring this book to life. As a Catholic boy and a believer, I couldn't omit an acknowledgement to Him for getting my "licence to live" renewed with each passing year.

Last but not least, I would like to dedicate this book to the memory of Terry Rawlings, the editor of *GoldenEye*, who died as I was writing these words. Without his sharp and effective work, I wouldn't have loved this film that much. May you rest in peace, Terry.

Nicolás Suszczyk,
Buenos Aires, May 2019

ABOUT THE BOOK

Complicated times for the James Bond fans reached an end on Wednesday, June 8, 1994. Times where the future of Bond was toughly questioned, where the character –absent from the screens since 1989– was considered dead, old-fashioned and not suitable for the 1990s. On that day, Pierce Brosnan was officially introduced as the new James Bond. Sporting a prominent beard and long hair and a dark suit, he greeted the world press giving the first step of what would later be known as *GoldenEye*, the 17th Bond onscreen adventure.

The Irish actor, born in 1953, was originally considered for the role in 1986, set to follow the steps of Roger Moore's Bond after *A View To A Kill*, released one year prior. Worldwide known in the 1980s for the leading role of the TV series *Remington Steele*, it was the renewal of this production that prevented him to star in *The Living Daylights*, where finally Timothy Dalton had his James Bond debut. Dalton would return for a second Bond movie, *Licence To Kill*, which was released in the Summer of 1989 to somewhat poor numbers in the box office.

Set for a 1995 release, *GoldenEye* took the name of Ian Fleming's estate in Jamaica, where he wrote all of his James Bond novels. It would be the first Bond production released after the Cold War, and the one that paved the way for the new millennium, and for a world which was getting every day smaller due to the emergence of the Internet and other technologies, increasing the speed and reach of global communications.

As we are heading to the 25th anniversary of *GoldenEye* next year, this book tries to take a closer look at the film, a comprehensive analysis to many of its aspects and an assessment of its legacy throughout these years. The study will begin with the man who started it all: Ian Fleming. There are perhaps little connections between this film and the original 007 novels penned in the 1950s, however the title for the film does come from Fleming and has been associated to an operation he carried away during World War II and his home in Jamaica, which became the place of Bond's inception.

The next thing to consider is *GoldenEye* in relation to the other James Bond films: what did Bond 17 brought to the franchise, why it is such an important entry in the saga, and what were the innovations that this production brought to the James Bond character in general. Since an event taking place during World War II serves as the villain's motivation for revenge against the British and the story itself deals very much with the new world order set in the 1990s, the next chapter will treat the connections between *GoldenEye* and the Cold War: what's old and new in the film, how the film is a bridge between old and new in world history.

The book continues by analysing the female companions of James Bond, detailing how the women of *GoldenEye* set a new standard for future Bond girls in the saga: characters like Natalya Simonova getting into Bond's mind or the appearance of the first female M, head of the British Intelligence, and the evolution of her somewhat motherly relationship with the secret agent throughout the franchise culminating in 2012's *Skyfall*.

The film's recurring theme of betrayal will also be examined in this book, starting with the primary example which is, of course, the relationship between agents 007 and 006, once friends and later declared enemies standing on different sides, with different ideas on patriotism and honour. And since *GoldenEye* brought a new generation of 007 fans for the 1990s, just like *Goldfinger* or *Thunderball* did in the 1960s, a chapter will focus on this so-called "GoldenEye Generation": how do they think, what kind of films they like and why do they vindicate this film so much. The place of *GoldenEye* as a 1990s blockbuster will also be considered in this study.

The success of the film relied on a very collaborative work between director Martin Campbell and the rest of the crew, so a chapter will explore the filmmaking process behind *GoldenEye*: the strikingly visual and cinematic approach given to the film and an international cast which was relatively unknown outside their countries of nationality, and yet they have delivered incredible performances.

Naturally, no study of *GoldenEye* would be complete without taking into consideration its many video game adaptations, which heavily increased the popularity of the film and the Bond series, particularly the Pierce Brosnan era. A chapter will revise the creative process behind these games and evaluate the impact of the name *GoldenEye* in the video gaming world.

The study ends with a conclusion on the legacy of *GoldenEye*, which was crucial to keep alive the legend of James Bond. A note on what the press said back in the day and how the movie is enormously celebrated by Bond fans and moviegoers nowadays, who rank it very high on their lists, considering it the best of the four Pierce Brosnan films in the role of the secret agent.

Regarding quotations: Every source taken from publications like books, magazines and web sites will be properly cited at the end of the book. Quotes taken from the film will not be referenced, just like declarations from people who got in touch with the author instead of being previously published elsewhere.

GOLDENEYE
AND IAN FLEMING

Before studying the great commercial impact of *GoldenEye* given by the 1995 film and its 1997 video game version, a huge consideration has to be made to the creator of Bond himself, Ian Fleming.

The film had no direct relation to any of his books or short stories, but it did have a relation to the place where he lived in every summer: Goldeneye, in Jamaica. Fleming, a journalist and then a member of Naval Intelligence, first went to Jamaica in 1942, during World War II with his friend Ivar Bryce. They both visited the Caribbean island attending to an Anglo-American conference to discuss the activities of the German U-boats, and Fleming stayed with Bryce and his second wife, who had a house in this paradisiac place. Fascinated with the island, he decided to build a house in Oracabessa, at the north of Jamaica, where he would live after the war and dedicate his life to do aquatic sports and write "the spy story to end all spy stories"[1], later known as *Casino Royale* which, in 1953, initiated the adventures of James Bond through a series of 14 books that inspired the films, which gave the character international recognition and acclaim. He called this house "Goldeneye".

According to author Matthew Parker, the name comes from "a wartime operation he had planned for the defence of Gibraltar, should Spain enter the war, and because of the happy coincidence that Oracabessa meant 'Golden Head' in Spanish."[2] In an interview published in 1965, Ian Fleming commented that he was reading Carson McCullers' 1941 novel *Reflections In a Golden Eye* when the house was complete, although Ivar Bryce and Fleming's wife Ann only cite the World War II operation and Oracabessa as the source where the name of this place was taken.[3] Carson McCullers' book is unrelated to the world of spying. It deals with an American private obsessed with the wife of his superior after seeing her naked. In 1967, a movie based on the book was released, directed by John Houston and starring Marlon Brando and Elizabeth Taylor.

Specific details of this World War II operation can be read on the book *Operation Golden Eye*, written by historian Mark Simmons, who briefly outlined it on an interview with the site *Artistic Licence Renewed*: "Operation Golden Eye was a stay-behind sabotage and disruption scheme to be implemented should the Germans have moved into Spain. It was subdivided into Operation Sconce if the Spanish co-operated with the Germans and Operation Sprinkler if they resisted. There was a similar scheme Operation Panicle for Portugal."[4]

The Goldeneye estate was finished by the end of 1946, following Ian Fleming's specifications: "Ten acres or so, away from towns and on the coast… there must be cliffs of some sort and a secret bay and no roads between the house and the shore"[5]. He lived there with his wife Anne Rothermere, who divorced press tycoon Esmond Rorthermere to marry Fleming, her long-time lover. They both spend the summer in the house and whenever they went back to London, Goldeneye was rented to notable people, like the famous playwright Noël Coward, the first of a list that included Truman Capote, Evelyn Waugh, Errol Flynn and Prime Minister Sir Anthony Eden, who went there to relax after his dealings with the Suez Crisis.

Ian Fleming was never used to the idea of getting married and avoided big social encounters every time he could. He found an escape room by carrying on with the idea that was for many years on the back of his mind: writing a thriller loosely based on his wartime experiences, which eventually became a series of books.

Just like Goldeneye, the name for this fictional spy would have a precedent in books: James Bond was an American ornithologist, author of *Birds of The West Indies*, a book Fleming consulted regularly. "I wanted the simplest, dullest, plainest-sounding name I could find (…) Exotic things would happen to and around him, but he would be a neutral figure —an anonymous, blunt instrument wielded by a government department,"[6] he explained. Funnily enough, Fleming met the real James Bond, who visited him in Jamaica. The creator of 007 jokingly apologised for the unauthorised use of his name. On a letter to Bond's wife, he wrote: "I can offer you unlimited use of the name Ian Fleming for any purposes you might think fit. Perhaps one day your husband will discover a particularly horrible species of bird which he would like to christen in an insulting fashion by calling it Ian Fleming."[7]

Almost a month before the release of *Goldfinger*, the film that launched the first waves of Bond mania all over the world, Ian Fleming died of a heart attack at the age of 56 on August 12, 1964. Nevertheless, his fascinating life would be fictionalized many times for the small screen between 1989 and 2014. Actors like Charles Dance, Jason Connery, Ben Daniels and Dominic Cooper would play the author in productions dedicated to his life or his work, like 2011's *Age of Heroes*, which narrates the creation of Fleming's 30 Assault Unit during World War II, under the command of one Major Jones (*GoldenEye*'s Sean Bean), where Fleming was played by James D'Arcy.

The Ian Fleming biopic which is considered to be most faithful to the author's life was directed by Don Boyd, based on John Pearson's biography *The Life of Ian Fleming*, and it also shares the title with Fleming's Jamaican house and, subsequently, with the 1995 film: *Goldeneye*.

Premiered on August 21, 1989, this TV adaptation sees Charles Dance in the role of Fleming, first seen at Goldeneye replicating the famous CBS interview in which he gives some details on the inception of his character. Future Bond alumni like Julian Fellowes (*Tomorrow Never Dies*) and Christoph Waltz (*SPECTRE*) also feature, the first one standing out in a very lively performance as playwright Noël Coward. This production suffers for slow pacing and low budgeted TV quality; but it undoubtedly characterises Ian Fleming's life better than any of the other productions, who tried to aim for a Bond-movie-like action/adventure production rather to the quieter story of his creator, who saw little action in the field and was much more of an operations planner. Needless to say, Charles Dance not only physically resembles Fleming very well, but he can quite provide the seductive traits and sense of humour attributed to his persona, plus the Intelligence experiences that later led to the development of James Bond.

The 1995 film *GoldenEye*, which is the object of study of this book, has no apparent relation to Ian Fleming and his character story-wise. However, amidst an original story that is set in a much different era, with new technologies applied to the field of spying, it should be noted that something of Fleming did sink in: The film poster tries to resemble the description of the literary Bond with a lock of his hair falling like "a thick comma above his right eyebrow"[8], and the scene where 007 tries to stop Alec Trevelyan's train by positioning his tank right in front of the locomotive and firing a shot from the cannon is somewhat reminiscent to the way Bond disables Serraffimo Spang's train in *Diamonds Are Forever*, the fourth Fleming novel published in 1956[9]. Likewise, the background of the villain Sir Hugo Drax, a British hero with a faced disfigured by bombings, plotting an attack against Great Britain in *Moonraker*[10], is quite similar to the one of Alec Trevelyan in the movie.

However, the most important situation that ties *GoldenEye* to Ian Fleming's James Bond is a reference to the secret agent's childhood, when Trevelyan remembers him that his parents "had the luxury of dying on a climbing accident". In Fleming's penultimate novel, *You Only Live Twice*, the author details the death of Bond's progenitors while trying to climb the

Aiguilles Rouges in Chamonix, France[11]. Future films like *Skyfall* and *SPECTRE* would also deal with the childhood of James Bond somehow, but *GoldenEye* has the distinction of being the first movie where this past is briefly disclosed.

GOLDENEYE
AND JAMES BOND

Back in the early 1990s, novelist John Gardner continued the literary version of James Bond and Domark released a number of video games starring the British spy. However, his absence from the big screen was sorely felt by the Bond fans between 1989 and 1995. The poor box office numbers of *Licence To Kill* and legal conflicts concerning Danjaq (the holding protecting the Bond copyright) with the businessmen taking over MGM/UA complicated the production of the seventeenth James Bond film[12]. Magazines named Timothy Dalton's last 007 outing as "James Bond's Final Mission"[13], and people assumed Ian Fleming's secret agent wouldn't be apt or get to survive this new and revolutionary decade. Luckily, the clouds cleared around 1992 and exactly on June 8, 1994, it was confirmed that James Bond would return in *GoldenEye*, starring Pierce Brosnan and set for a 1995 release. The casting of Brosnan, who missed the Bond opportunity in 1986 due to contractual obligations with *Remington Steele*, pleased many cinemagoers and the expectancy was high. But even as the machine was set in motion, a question had to be answered: Are people still interested in James Bond?

GoldenEye answered this question affirmatively and it did not only demonstrate that 007 was still relevant, but the character became the goose that laid the golden eggs for United Artists, the original 007 movie studio now under MGM's holdings. "MGM/UA realized Bond was its most bankable asset so they pushed for more films as quickly as possible,"[14] pointed out Jeff Kleeman, the company's vice-president during most of the 1990s, on an interview with *The Secret Agent Lair*. He also noted that *GoldenEye*'s success was fundamental to bring the following Brosnan-Bond films *Tomorrow Never Dies* and *The World Is Not Enough* in 1997 and 1999, respectively, and later *Die Another Day* in 2002[15].

Now, what is *GoldenEye* to the James Bond franchise, overall? Does it share elements tying it to the previous outings or is it a completely reinvented James Bond, exclusively aimed for a new generation? Is the film a classic? Let's take a look at the film, backwards…

GoldenEye was the James Bond film that saved the franchise and guaranteed its continuity in the 1990s and the 21st century, for sure. Reflecting on the film in *The Digital Bits*, Ian Fleming Foundation's founding member John Cork pointed out that "*GoldenEye* proved all the doubters wrong. Bond's continued relevance, it turned out, had little to do with Cold War politics or studio equity. It had everything to do with quality. Everyone involved in making *GoldenEye* was hungry, and it shows (...) Had *GoldenEye* failed, that would have been it for 007. The stakes with the film were incredibly high."[16] Analysed to a bigger extent, the seventeenth Bond adventure meant an improvement over the somewhat monotonous quality of the five earlier Bond movies, directed by John Glen, who has previously been the editor and second unit director in films like *On Her Majesty's Secret Service* and *The Spy Who Loved Me*.

Commanded by New Zealand-born director Martin Campbell, *GoldenEye* brought fresh air to a franchise that was becoming a bit repetitive and unglamorous.

Between 1981 and 1989, Glen did an amazing job in what it comes to tone down the slapstick humour and place Bond in down-to-earth stories, but the acclaimed visual quality that characterized the Bond films for decades has been notoriously depreciated, feeling like made-for-TV action movies at times. The cinematography by Alan Hume and Alec Mills was often mild in comparison to the job carried away by Phil Méheux, whose visual impact was achieved through breath-taking establishing shots and detailed close-ups for many of the character reactions. The team behind *GoldenEye* brought back that visual, cinematic quality that characterized James Bond in the 1960s, which was greatly missed in the 1980s. "I wanted to get back more to the (Sean) Connery-type stories. I wanted to make it grittier, slightly more based on reality than they have been in the past"[17], noted Campbell, quoted in *The James Bond Archives*.

However, *GoldenEye* does owe something to the John Glen films: the big development of action sequences. The aerial stunts featured in *Octopussy* and *The Living Daylights*, or the thrilling vehicle chase involving tankers through the Mexican desert in *Licence To Kill* did set a precedent for some action moments in the 1995 film, like the opening sequence where Bond catches a plane mid-air or the epic tank chase through the streets of St. Petersburg. Martin Campbell (and his second unit director, Ian Sharp) combined the exhilarating vehicle chases from the

John Glen movies with the dynamic approach of the Terence Young ones. The glamour and colourful visuals of the film are also very reminiscent to Guy Hamilton, who, along with other three films, directed the most popular James Bond movie, *Goldfinger*. This effective combination turned out into a very exciting film for adrenaline lovers.

GoldenEye also tried to establish Pierce Brosnan as a spiritual heir to Sean Connery, widely recognised by many as the quintessential James Bond. This way, Brosnan is the first actor since Connery to drive the iconic silver Aston Martin DB5 –number plate BMT 214A opposed to BMT 216A as the *Goldfinger* machine– last seen thirty years earlier in the introductory sequence of *Thunderball*. Also, just like Connery in *Dr No*, Brosnan first says his "Bond, James Bond" introduction to a woman in a casino. The replicated casino scene in *GoldenEye* even has the daughter of the late Eunice Gayson, who played Sylvia Trench in the aforementioned scene from *Dr No*, making a small cameo role as one of the guests. But despite these connections to Connery, Pierce Brosnan set a unique standard for the character which was quite different from the portrayal of the original 007: a vulnerable Bond.

Director Martin Campbell told *Cinefantastique* that "Pierce has brought his own contemporary and personal sides to the character. There's a depth in the *GoldenEye* Bond that I always thought was missing from other entries in the series. Pierce has lifted Bond above the superficial."[18] In retrospect, it is evident that what Campbell said goes beyond doing publicity for his movie and he truly has a point when talking about the depth of Bond's persona in *GoldenEye*.

Timothy Dalton had some dramatic reactions in *Licence To Kill*, particularly as he sees the maimed body of his friend Felix Leiter, severely injured by a shark attack. Still, Brosnan's portrayal was the first that allowed audiences to get a little into James Bond's mind as he wonders about the nature of his job and the fact that he will confront someone who was a close friend, in a scene which very akin to the first chapter of Ian Fleming's 1959 novel *Goldfinger*, where he reflects on the man he just killed, a Mexican hitman[19]. Moments later, the villain will evaluate Bond's attitudes: "I might as well ask you if all the vodka martinis ever silence the screams of all the men you've killed. Or if you find forgiveness in the arms of all those willing women for all the dead ones you failed to protect," a direct allusion to Tracy Di Vicenzo, Bond's ill-fated wife in *On Her Majesty's Secret Service*. Situations like this would be regular in the Daniel Craig's James Bond adventures beginning in 2006 with *Casino Royale*.

With his James Bond portrayal, the Irish actor has achieved to reunite the best qualities of each of his predecessors: Connery's irony and strength, some of Moore's sense of humour and the human side of Lazenby and Dalton, and yet he offered the character a uniquely human side, that doesn't prevent him to also act cool or deadly in different situations. Talking to the world press right after being appointed as the new James Bond, Pierce Brosnan emphasised he wanted to "see what is beneath the surface of this man, what drives him on, what makes him a killer"[20]. This would be a regular claim by Brosnan throughout his era, and although most of the films deviated into action movies with more entertainment than drama, none of them was without a few minutes where Bond was given an introspective approach: notably Paris Carver's death in *Tomorrow Never Dies*, the betrayal of Elektra King in *The World Is Not Enough* and the MI6 abandonment he suffers after his 14 month captivity in a North Korean prison in *Die Another Day*. In the end, Brosnan showed that is great to be Bond, but at the same time that being him is not all fun and games as it was in the days of Connery or Moore.

Despite the many new things a James Bond for the '90s would have to offer in order to be attractive to new audiences, *GoldenEye* is very respectful to the original blueprint of most Bond films. It begins with the iconic gun barrel sequence (given a digital CGI makeup), opens up with an explosive introductory action scene, then we are led to the main titles filled with beautiful women posing over the credits and iconography related to the main plot, and there are more or less of the classic 007 elements: beautiful Bond girls (the good girl, the bad girl and the occasional "conquest"), a villain with a plan that could put the world or England in danger, and of course the happy ending between Bond and the leading girl, generally with a hint of humour. At the same time, there are the usual scenes that the audience had grown accustomed to: Bond flirting with Moneypenny, being debriefed by M and getting his gadgets from Q.

The most significant changes in these scenes come from the interactions between Bond with Moneypenny and M, which has been now made a woman to reflect Stella Rimmington's appointment as the head of MI5 in 1992. These roles were played by Samantha Bond (her surname is purely a coincidence) and noted British actress Judi Dench, and the dynamics between 007 and these well-known characters of the series have been modified: Moneypenny isn't desperate for Bond and she is a bit cold at his advances, while the new M is also very strict with him but in a more feminist and bureaucratic way in contrast to Bernard Lee's portrayal as a Royal Navy Admiral. What hasn't changed at all and looks incredibly familiar to the previous Bond films is the famous Q scene, starting with the actor who portrays the MI6 gadget master, Desmond Llewelyn. Q is as impatient and as grouch with 007 as he has always been, asking him to "return this equipment in pristine order" and to "grow up!" The structure of the film helps to blend in both the new elements with the classic elements in a seamless way, accomplishing the task to please Bond fans of different ages. So, in that sense, *GoldenEye* is indeed a "classic", or at the very least, a "classic James Bond film".

The movie also reworks some of the best moments in the series, particularly in some action scenes that bring back old memories to previous entries: the hand-to-hand combat between 007 and Trevelyan has the same intensity and brutality as that confrontation in the Orient Express between Bond and Red Grant in *From Russia With Love*, or the close quarters combat between Bond and Peter Franks inside an elevator in

Diamonds Are Forever. Equally, the sauna confrontation between Bond and Xenia is a steamier version of Bond "practising judo" with Pussy Galore in a haystack in *Goldfinger* and the domino-like fall of cyclists in Monaco after the Aston Martin and Ferrari pass them by at an outrageous speed is similar to a scene from *For Your Eyes Only*, done with skiers in Cortina d'Ampezzo. With Trevelyan's hideout underneath an inconspicuous looking river among the jungle, production designer Peter Lamont tributes Ken Adam's *You Only Live Twice* set of Ernst Stavro Blofeld's lair hidden inside an inactive volcano in Japan. So, indeed, all of the "classic" trademark Bond situations can be seen in *GoldenEye* only that readapted for this new decade.

The John Gardner novels also appeared to inspire *GoldenEye* a little, since there are moments in the film that seem (perhaps by chance) a bit reminiscent to the pages of some of Gardner's original stories: the way Bond meets Xenia Onatopp in Monte Carlo is similar to his encounter with Percy Proud in the 1984 book *Role of Honour*, not to mention the fact that this woman is a computer expert much like Natalya Simonova was in *GoldenEye*[21]. At the same time, in 1982's *For Special Services*, SPECTRE plots to infiltrate a space weapons facility on the Cheyenne Mountain by having a senior officer using his authority to perform an unscheduled test[22]. This might have inspired Ourumov's attack on Severnaya or Michael France's original script where the basis for what would eventually become this scene was set right after the pre-credits sequence. The 1991 novel *The Man From Barbarossa* also shares some links with *GoldenEye*: the villain,

Russian General Yevgeny Yuskovich, schemes the stage of a fake trial against a war criminal –presumed to be part of the Babi Yar massacre from 1941– to divert people from his real intentions, which consist of arming the Iraqis to sabotage *perestroika*, throw the current government away and place himself as the leader of a new Soviet government[23]. In the 1995 film, General Ourumov sees himself as "the next Iron Man of Russia", had a participation in the 1991 coup against Mikhail Gorbachov, and forges an allegiance with the Janus Syndicate, known for having restocked the Iraqis after the Gulf War, or so Bond says.

A key point of *GoldenEye* is the film's many action scenes, which are among the best of the series and perhaps one step ahead of the older films, even those that one has to sometimes dare to question: the escape from captivity in the Military Archives building in St. Petersburg, with Bond shooting his way out (a sequence masterfully edited by Terry Rawlings) is something that is perhaps equalled to the Piz Gloria assault in *On Her Majesty's Secret Service*, and yet difficult to top. Not to mention the tank chase over St. Petersburg, with Bond destroying half the city with a T55 Russian tank in pursuit of General Ourumov.

Characteristics like this place *GoldenEye* as one of the best James Bond films ever made: the combination between the directorial style of Terence Young, Guy Hamilton and John Glen which resulted on a quality rarely seen again in the franchise until perhaps *Casino Royale*, which was also directed by Martin Campbell to introduce Daniel Craig as James Bond. And even when the Craig era tried to offer a more brutal and less escapist

Bond than the one we saw in *GoldenEye*, films like *Skyfall* and *SPECTRE* seemed to acknowledge some bits of the movie: the first one with a renegade MI6 agent plotting against England, the latter with a villain linked to Bond's past that was presumed dead before revealing himself as the mastermind behind it all. The two Sam Mendes films also mention an exploding pen (a gadget that saved 007's life in *GoldenEye*) and feature an aerial stunt with a helicopter which was very much similar to the one seen at the pre-credits of *GoldenEye* as Bond escapes from Soviet troops in Arkangel by catching a Pilatus aeroplane in mid-air.

Crucial for the success of *GoldenEye* was also its marketing campaign, which urged to publicise that James Bond was back with all the traditional elements that have made the franchise successful. After the somewhat lacklustre poster campaign for *Licence To Kill*, with Timothy Dalton in an unglamorous black shirt in a *Die Hard* vibe, *GoldenEye* brought back the poster artwork glory for James Bond by taking advantage of the latest cutting-edge digital photomontage techniques.

Using photographs from a session taken by John Stoddart and stills credited to Terry O'Neill and Keith Hamshere, art directors Randi Braun and Earl Klaski created an innovative campaign which combined the striking contrast between black, red, gold and yellow for both the American and international theatrical posters, and the new Bond prominently flanked by his female companions as a collage of the best moments of the film surround them. These posters were preceded by other two "Advance" versions that emphasised that James Bond was back: a zoom-in of the secret agent's eye aiming his Walther PPK handgun for the United States and a more conventional image of Pierce Brosnan in tuxedo making a classical pose under the film's tagline: "You know the name. You know the number".

No less impressive was the film's teaser trailer: "It's a new world, with new threats and new enemies. But you can still depend on one man", it read as the new Bond walked to the camera and, breaking the fourth wall, asked to the audiences: "You were expecting someone else?" Then, the highlight of the film's action sequences flashed onscreen over a new rendition of the "James Bond Theme" performed by Starr Parodi and Jeff Fair, which was highly acclaimed by the fans all over the world: "It's great that so many of the Bond fans connected with the piece," reflected the married duo of musicians on a 2013 interview with *The GoldenEye Dossier*. "It was a tremendous honour to work on and the fans were really the ones that got the *GoldenEye* Trailer Bond Theme music on the *Best of Bond* CD by sending so many requests to MGM for the music."[24] On an article in *Forbes*, critic Scott Mendelson observed that the teaser trailer for *GoldenEye* "reinvented the modern action movie trailer and slowly-but-surely changed how trailers for action movies were constructed" and that "it was arguably the first trailer to move so quickly that you could barely digest the images, (…) perhaps the most action-packed and relentlessly breathless action movie trailer you had ever seen."[25]

The trailers of *GoldenEye* have also revealed that in the film Bond will be facing "the man who knows him better: 006". This may look surprising in an era where moviegoers and fans are cautious of reading spoilers or knowing important (sometimes, hardly important) parts of the plot, although even the track listing of many Bond soundtracks have revealed the fate of some of the characters in the past. Reflecting on the film's promotion, Jeff Kleeman explained: "We felt the idea of 006 vs. 007 was a selling point. It was a way to bring people back to Bond and introduce new audiences to Bond. It's a tiny spoiler that we felt didn't ruin the experience of watching the movie."[26]

Another important part of the marketing campaign included deals with well-known companies to tie-in James Bond to their products. The most notable was Omega, who initiated a long relationship as 007's wristwatch provider with *GoldenEye* and is still associated with the character. Also, for the first time, Bond sat behind the wheel of a blue BMW Z3 Roadster, which hadn't been officially launched at the time of filming. The deal was done after a visit from the producers to BMW's design centre in 1994 in Munich and the cooperation was announced in January 1995, right as the film started production. The appearance of the car was an extremely well-kept secret and only a brown shipping container stood up for the vehicle, between Bond's classic Aston Martin DB5 and Xenia's Ferrari 355. BMW provided two handmade pre-production models for the shooting of the film in Puerto Rico (doubling for Cuba) and they were heavily guarded to avoid anyone taking pictures before the official announcement, although somehow some candid shots leaked to the press[27]. Finally, the car was formally presented by Desmond Llewelyn on November 13, 1995, in New

York, just before the film's premiere later that day[28]. Brands like Perrier, Kodak, IBM and Smirnoff also jumped into the "Bond-wagon".

Taking in more than 352 million dollars worldwide, *GoldenEye* was the most successful Bond film since 1979's *Moonraker* and brought a new fan base to the world: those were the millions of kids and teens who were asking their parents "who that James Bond guy was", as they discovered that four actors have played the role before Pierce Brosnan through 16 films since 1962 and that the phenomenon included books, comics and video games and lots of merchandising to collect.

In other words, *GoldenEye* did not only save James Bond, but it was also the holy water that christened and initiated many people into the Bond mania.

GOLDENEYE
AND THE COLD WAR

The new M, a female analyst played by Judi Dench, calls James Bond "a relic of the Cold War" in *GoldenEye*. Characters like CIA agent Jack Wade and former KGB agent Valentin Zukovsky typecast Bond as an old-fashioned guy, a man with no place in the 1990s. All over the world, back then, there was also an archetypical vision of Bond as the number one enemy of Mother Russia. And he was indeed during the first Ian Fleming's novels, where Bond swore to defeat SMERSH –the brutal execution branch of the Soviet Union– in 1953's *Casino Royale*. However, as noted by James Chapman in his book *Licence to Thrill: A Cultural History of the James Bond Films*, the Bond movies avoided to interfere with the hot political climate of the 1960s and the Russians usually ended up being used for fools by an apolitical organization like SPECTRE (*Dr No*, *From Russia With Love, You Only Live Twice*), a renegade Soviet General (*Octopussy*) or the communist faction of the Far East (*Goldfinger* and *Dr. No* again, with the leading villains in league or coming from the Red China)[29].

Before *GoldenEye*, the only times Bond has really antagonized with the Russians was in *For Your Eyes Only* and *The Living Daylights*, in 1981 and 1987, respectively. The first film dealt with the disappearance of an electronic device from a sunken British spy ship in Albania, which the Russians are eager to obtain. Near the end of the film, Bond shows some *détente* and destroys it before KGB's General Gogol could obtain it ("You don't have it, I don't have it", quips 007 as both men start to laugh). In the second film, a training mission in Gibraltar is infiltrated by a SMERSH agent who murders 004. Things turn nastier when General Koskov, a Russian defector, is kidnapped in British soil. Bond is initially sent to terminate General Pushkin, the man who apparently ordered the conspiracy against the British Intelligence. However, before Bond can pull the trigger, Pushkin informs him that Koskov is behind it all and he's in league with Brad Whitaker, an American mercenary, in arms dealing scheme. Once again, the Soviet Union was not the enemy after all.

Being the first film released after the fall of the Berlin Wall, *GoldenEye* deals heavily with the passing of time, which is continuously referenced in the story. The beginning of the film is set in 1986, with (in a rare sense of poetic justice) Pierce Brosnan "sneaking" into Timothy Dalton's timeline[30].

Agent 007 joins Alec Trevelyan, agent 006, to "save the world again" on a mission to a nerve gas facility in Arkangel, in the north of the Soviet Union. Trevelyan is captured by General Ourumov and killed in front of Bond, who successfully escapes before blowing the place to bits. This is followed by Daniel Kleinman's main title sequence, played over Tina Turner's title theme, as scantily clad women destroy Soviet statues. The title sequence, in fact, offended some Communist territories and the film wasn't shown because of that. On a 2013 interview with *The GoldenEye*

Dossier, Kleinman remembers the controversy and defended his work: "Statues really were torn down, as is seen later in the movie, and although it wasn't literally girls in lingerie who caused icons to fall and the Soviet State to break up, in an analogous way perhaps it was. The Soviet people wanted what the west had: goods and glamour. Remember, not that long time before then people had been smuggling in Levi's."[31]

After the main titles, we are in the present day. There are no references to precise years or dates, but the pre-credits sequence presents Bond as a crusader against a mischievous Russian General and potential terrorist, the main titles describe the fall of the Berlin wall and the setting of a new world order, and then we are here in 1995: "Nine years later", we see superimposed on the bottom of the screen as James Bond drives his Aston Martin DB5 through Monte Carlo.

The first draft of *GoldenEye*, penned by screenwriter and long-time Bond fan Michael France, was delivered on April 1994. The Cold War and the antagonism between Great Britain and Russia were very present in the story, much more than what it was in the final film. After KGB defector Anatoly Razhnov, a scientist working on England, was "neutralised" by a suspicious neurotoxin, Bond is sent to Moscow. He has a prickly encounter with *The Living Daylights*' General Pushkin in a reception, suspecting the KGB was behind the attack. As he's invited to leave, he encounters Augustus Trevelyan, a former MI6 agent and a mentor for Bond in the old days. Trevelyan was presumed dead for a long time, but he has actually defected to Russia after betraying Bond and fellow agents 003 and 005 during a rescue operation. He has been given diplomatic status, and placed in charge of a secret execution branch similar to SMERSH, with one of his tasks being the order on the attack against Razhnov. His ultimate target would be New York's World Trade Center instead of the Bank of England, again ultimately aiming at personal profit[32].

"The problem with my draft was that there was far *too* much action. Wall-to-wall action. Every ten minutes you had a $20 million sequence"[33], admitted France, explaining one of the reasons for the changes suffered by his original script. Scribes Jeffrey Caine and Bruce Feirstein, with the intervention of Kevin Wade, reworked most of the story by toning down the political aspects and the antagonism with Russia, as they also came up with new characters, scrapped out some action scenes and added new ones. The story was also adjusted to Pierce Brosnan's performance since France wrote his draft thinking of Timothy Dalton, who by that time dropped from the role feeling the delay of the film would compromise his other projects[34]. Another significant change was made in the antagonist, Trevelyan, turned into a much younger agent with more or less the same age as Bond, and more of a trusty friend than an older mentor who trained him.

This new Trevelyan was renamed Alec and had no diplomatic immunity from the Russian government. Presumed dead, he operated in the shadows in the arms dealing business (arming the Iraqis after the Gulf War) as the mysterious head of the Janus Syndicate. Trevelyan's number one ally was none other than his "executioner" himself, General Ourumov, who embodies pretty much of the old world order and Soviet Russia. His patriotism resembles General G., the SMERSH leader in Ian Fleming's *From Russia With Love* novel[35]. German actor Gottfried John, who played Ourumov, noted to author Garth Pearce that his character "is a traditional Russian General who tries to re-establish the old system while using the new Russian mafia to do so" and that "he thinks he can win the battle but becomes like a trapped animal"[36]. This character –and his pact with Trevelyan– is particularly interesting to analyse because it connects the movie with the Cold War and the inception of the new world order, which saw the emergence of a new Russia.

According to the MI6 files, briefly glimpsed on M's computer in the film, Ourumov was "made a General" and given the command of the Space Division in the early 1990s, years after his first encounter with Bond in the pre-credits. It is believed, according to the same file, that he was one of the conspirators behind the Soviet coup d'état attempt against Mikhail Gorbachev in August 1991, but after the suicide of a co-conspirator, the inquiry against him was dropped.

Between 1986 and 1995, Ourumov went from being a high ranking Soviet Colonel to be a General in charge of a government division, but he is noticeably uncomfortable on being under the orders of civilians, a reason to join the Janus Syndicate hoping to regain power and to bring back the glory days of the Soviet Union. One of his major political threats is Dimitri Mishkin, the Defence Minister brought by the democratic Boris Yeltsin administration[37]. A politician who, according to actor Tcheky

Karyo, "fights against the military trying to take over Russia"[38]. This way, General Ourumov is "a trapped animal" between the new forces ruling his country: Mishkin and the politicians, part of this new, democratic Russia naturally opposed to people like Ourumov; and the mafias like the Janus Syndicate, who promised him "more money than God" and –eventually– to regain political power in a similar fashion to *Octopussy*'s General Orlov, brilliantly played by Steven Berkoff.

The sense of an anachronism does not extend only to General Ourumov but to James Bond himself. They both belong to the old world order where armies or spies fought each other for ideologies and patriotism. "Are you still working for MI6, or have you decided to join the 21st century?" scoffs ex KGB agent Valentin Zukovsky when his former enemy, Bond, pays him a visit in order to set up a meeting with Janus. Much like Ourumov, Zukovsky was another knight of Mother Russia who has now joined the dark side as an arms dealer and the direct competitor to Janus in that illegal business. Characters like Zukovsky and Trevelyan contrast with Bond's patriotism and devotion for Queen and Country: an old-fashioned feeling, an antiquated idea shared by a military man like Ourumov, but his ambition for power ("He sees himself as the new Iron Man of Russia", M comments) has made him shake his hands with the Devil, or in this case, the Janus Syndicate.

Ironically, the same pressure Ourumov feels from the politicians overseeing the military is –in a minor sense– felt by James Bond, reluctant to accept the new M, a civilian (aka "The Evil Queen of Numbers") who replaced the old Admiral Sir Miles Messervy commanding the British Secret Service in the previous entries. The new MI6 Headquarters, a not-so-secret building on the banks of the Thames River next to Vauxhall Bridge, is now a technological facility with computers, laptops, electronic doors and satellite screens much more different than the conservative looking office of the old M, decorated with wood furniture and paintings of naval battles. The future is here and Bond isn't too keen on a "bean counter" (and a woman) running the British Intelligence. So, in this sense, both Bond and Ourumov are opposite sides of the same coin: both "trapped animals" in a new world.

Although Alec Trevelyan is interested in making money, his main interest is clearly revenge. As he reencounters with Bond in an abandoned Soviet statue park late at night, Trevelyan reveals to him that he was alive and switched sides: "We're both orphans, James. But where your parents had the luxury of dying in a climbing accident, mine survived the British betrayal and Stalin's execution squads."

The story of Trevelyan's parents is linked to an event taking place by the end of World War II when a group of Cossacks led by General Piotr Krasnov had betrayed the Red Army and joined the Nazis to fight them. After the triumph of the Russians, Krasnov persuaded Hitler in 1944 to settle in the Alps, where they kicked their inhabitants out and established garrisons, churches and other buildings. The Allied would ultimately advance from Italy to the Italian Alps, forcing these Cossacks to establish in Lienz, Austria. Once there, the British interned the Cossacks in a camp before the promise to take them to a conference with their officers, probably to arrange some kind of a deal. Ultimately, in 1945, the British betrayed the Cossacks and handed them back to the Soviet Union. Their fate was sealed after the Yalta conference between Stalin, Roosevelt and Churchill, the first assuring the latter that these Cossacks fought with ferocity for the Germans. Krasnov and other high-ranking officers were tried and sentenced to death by hanging, while others –like Trevelyan's parents– committed suicide after escaping from Stalin's execution squads[39].

Earlier in the film, Valentin Zukovsky briefly narrates the Lienz betrayal to Bond, to what the secret agent admits with a pinch of guilt that it wasn't Britain's "finest hour", referencing Churchill's 1940 public speech to the House of Commons[40]. Zukovsky, on the other hand, and probably in allusion to Stalin's words on the Cossack's savagery, points out that these people were "ruthless" and "got what they deserved".

Bond would later wonder how MI6 didn't check the Lienz background on Trevelyan's past, to what he answers by detailing the reason behind his bitterness: "They knew. (...) MI6 figured I was too young to remember. And in one of life's little ironies, the son went to work for the government whose betrayal caused the father to kill himself and his wife."

Trevelyan also acknowledges Bond's old-fashioned patriotism: "I did think of asking you to join my little scheme, but somehow I knew 007's loyalty was always to the mission, never to his friend." Moreover, in John Gardner's novelization of the film script, the treacherous 006 gives a more lengthy explanation on the reason why he changed sides, also trivializing James Bond's patriotic values: "Trust has disappeared, gone, dropped out of the dictionary (...) It's all money. We're stuck in the slough of despond which goes under a new name: free market morality. It's a morality where your friends come and go as quickly as the next bus in Regent Street or Fifth Avenue"[41].

This fact is also connoted, production-wise, by placing the encounter in this old statue park where statues of Lenin, Stalin and Felix Dzerzhinsky (creator of the Soviet secret police) had been destroyed and torn down after the fall of the Berlin Wall. Juxtaposing Bond's imperialist values, the Soviet ideology embraced by people like Ourumov has also been overridden by money-makers, crime, corruption and mafias. Alec Trevelyan perfectly understands that the patriotic values of Bond and Ourumov are now old-fashioned and scraped out by "free market morality".

Ultimately, Trevelyan's revenge plan against Britain consists of detonating the GoldenEye weapon (consisting of two satellites, Petya and Mischa) over London. The EMP blast caused by this weapon, stolen by General Ourumov and Janus' accomplice Xenia Onatopp after massacring innocent employees in the Space Weapon Control Centre in Severnaya, will disable every computer in the City of London, erasing the records of every transfer that he has been doing hours before taking Britain to "the Stone Age" and making them "learn the cost of betrayal, inflation-adjusted to 1945",. That was the year, of course, where Trevelyan's parents were betrayed and committed suicide. Unlike Ourumov, Trevelyan is not a fervent Soviet or communist in terms of ideology, and his plan is more oriented to revenge and money-making. He also wants to humiliate Bond, who decided to carry on with the mission after Trevelyan was captured and "killed" in the gas plant, nine years before. While the execution of the former 006 was staged, Bond readjusted the timers of the explosives to three minutes instead of six; causing Trevelyan's to have half of his face scarred under the effects of the detonation and gas leaks. On a production minute, United Artists noted that audiences react well to villains with facial disfigurements[42].

The preliminary production notes of *GoldenEye* aimed straight to the concern of James Bond's continuity into the 1990s and the new world order: "The Hammer and Sickle was quickly and quietly replaced by Organised Crime - with Russia the epicentre of a new European Mafia whose tentacles are now spreading across the world with social, economic and occasionally violent repercussions. It is against this background that the latest James Bond adventure (...) is set."[43] The premise was no different to older Bond films where the Cold War had an important influence in the plot, but this time Russia was the battleground and the new political direction of the country was a pivotal aspect of the story.

It begins with the pre-credit sequence where 007 and 006 "save the world again" from the Soviet Union and their nerve gas arsenal in charge of a Russian Colonel. Then, Bond spots a Georgian woman in Monte Carlo which turns out to be a former Soviet fighter pilot who is tied to a Russian crime syndicate, Janus, who operated during the early 1990s in the arms dealing business. The woman steals an EMP hardened helicopter from a French warship and, aided by the aforementioned Colonel (now a General), steals a space weapon from a control centre in Severnaya and uses one of the satellites to target that station. Bond, who failed to prevent the theft of the helicopter, is sent to St. Petersburg to investigate every possible lead on the Janus Syndicate and its shadowy leader. As he arrives at the city, he finds the new Russia, once the country he went occasionally "shoot in and out" in the old days, which is now...

- "A land of opportunities", according to Xenia Onatopp, the aforementioned Soviet pilot member of the Janus Syndicate who enjoys a Ferrari F355 that "belongs to a friend".

- Crowded by the Russian mafia, who sends people back home "in very small boxes", as CIA's Jack Wade points out, integrated by people like Valentin Zukovsky and Alec Trevelyan, former spies now making money for themselves with arms dealing business ("You don't find this guy, he finds you").

- A country where, despite the changes, "the penalty for terrorism is still death", or so says Defence Minister Dimitri Mishkin to his captive Bond, framed by Janus as the man who stole the Tiger helicopter and took the GoldenEye weapon.

These descriptions of the new Russia by the characters of the film are also accompanied by another insurgence of capitalism in what was once the heart of Communism: personal computers and the Internet. The upbringings of the new technologies are laid out by two young characters: Natalya Simonova and Boris Grishenko, programmers working at Severnaya before the attack led by Ourumov and Onatopp. The first one is a moderate and conservative employee while the other is a geek who extremely confident of his talents and has zero respect for authority, bluntly yelling "I am invincible!" after hacking the web site of the US Department of Justice. Grishenko's ambition will place him under the wings of Janus and betray his workmates. On the other hand, Simonova will manage to hide from the burst of Xenia Onatopp's machine gun and later survive the multiple explosions detonated by the GoldenEye satellites, becoming a dangerous witness for Janus' plan and whose knowledge of computer science will be crucial for Bond to foil the enemy plan.

However, it should be important to note that Bond isn't precisely in good terms with the new Russian administration either: "Governments change, the lies stay the same," he tells M as she informs him that the Russian government told the Prime Minister that the two fighter MiG planes destroyed by the GoldenEye blast had "an accident during a routine training exercise". He also questions the apparent complicity between the new government and some high-ranking members of the old regime: "What's the penalty for treason?!" he asks the Defence Minister who reminds him that terrorists are still sentenced to the capital punishment. Once again, John Gardner expands the political references much more, making Bond's accusation more explicit: "What's the penalty for treason these days, Minister? A slap on the wrist and banishment to a country dacha, like the traitors who bungled the coup in '91?" Then, Mishkin clarifies that some have died and Bond notes: "Supposedly by their own hand" [44] as if he tried to mean that some of the conspirators were killed by someone else to avoid loose ends. Given that it was never proved that Ourumov was linked to the '91 coup due to the suicide of a co-conspirator, there is a possibility that this co-conspirator was silenced for good, perhaps with the help of Janus as they forged an alliance in the late 1980s or early 1990s.

The Cold War and the beginning of a new era is an essential subject in the world of *GoldenEye*, which in a way served as a farewell to the old James Bond films that embraced the subject or Russia on the other side of the field as "enemies". The passing of an era is reflected by characters, scenarios and the implementation of new technologies, which redefined the future of James Bond and made him relevant in the 1990s, preparing him to confront the threats of the new millennium and the post-9/11 era with films like *Die Another Day* and the 2006 reboot of *Casino Royale*.

GOLDENEYE
AND THE FEMALE AUTHORITY

It's an old and well-known publicity strategy to have every Bond girl – or at least most of the leading actresses of the James Bond films– to introduce their roles as a "Bond's equal" or "different to the other Bond girls". To affirm or deny this fact requires analysing that character in particular and comparing it to previous similar characters, but first, the exact meaning of "Bond girl" has to be defined. What is, exactly, a "Bond girl" or a "Bond woman"? Is it just an attractive actress making an appearance on a Bond film? A woman who gets a romantic interlude with James Bond? Or simply any female character/actress appearing on a James Bond movie?

There is also the fact that there are many kinds of female characters that partnered with Bond since the first movies: there is the damsel in distress type (Solitaire in *Live And Let Die*, for example), the occasional conquest (Sylvia Trench in *Dr No* and *From Russia With Love*), and the self-reliant heroines or villainess, like Melina Havelock in *For Your Eyes Only* or Fiona Volpe in *Thunderball*. A passing mention should also receive the beautiful women who are there just to sexually appeal the audience but have little to no romantic interaction with Bond, namely the gipsy fighting girls Vida and Zora in *From Russia With Love* or the female crowd gasping at 007's acrobatics over the Tangier rooftops in *The Living Daylights*.

In *GoldenEye*, the relationship between Bond and "his" women are defined through five female characters, independently if they have a romance with him or not: Caroline, the therapist sent by MI6 to re-evaluate him for active service; Xenia Onatopp, the former Soviet agent now allied with Janus; Miss Moneypenny, secretary of M; the new M, an analyst leading the British Secret Service; and Natalya Simonova, a computer programmer targeted by Janus who reluctantly joins him.

Screenwriter Bruce Feirstein reworked the female characters written by Michael France, Marina Varoskaya (the computer technician) and Xenia Labyakova (Trevelyan's assassin) into the two most prominent female characters of the film: the good girl Natalya Simonova and the bad girl Xenia Onatopp, whose name was given by Feirstein for her penchant for crushing men to death with her tights during lovemaking.

The New Jersey-born writer gave Natalya more relevance, turning her into a more active and self-reliant character, contradicting the idea that Bond girls were helpless bimbos who couldn't do anything without Bond by their side. As a matter of fact, Ian Fleming heroines like Dominetta Vitali (*Thunderball*) and Gala Brand (*Moonraker*) did oppose this common thinking of the Bond girls being irrelevant in the story, although most of the early adventures relied more on their seductive looks than to their actual importance in the story. Natalya may not be the most glamorous Bond girl of all –her wardrobe is quite boring, perhaps the most boring in the series–, but she will always be remembered for setting a precedent to future female characters that have been romantically involved with Bond: getting inside the hero's mind and allowing some introspection of him for the audience. Perhaps the first women that come to mind when it comes to thinking of a heroine conceived as a vehicle to let Bond open up and express his emotions are Vesper Lynd (Eva Green in *Casino Royale*) and Madeleine Swann (Léa Seydoux in *SPECTRE* and on the upcoming Bond 25), but it was Natalya Simonova the first one to let us see a little through Bond's mind in *GoldenEye*.

Sitting on a Cuban beach before his final confrontation with Trevelyan, his former friend, Bond is on a reflexive mood. In John Gardner's novelization, his thoughts are satisfactorily laid out for the readers:

> "What had he become, he asked himself. Was he just a killing machine? Did his superiors let him get away with all kinds of excesses both on and off missions because they understood the kind of strain his work produced? He knew that some people turned a blind eye to certain aspects of his way of life, just as he knew that they paid him more than most of the regular officers of the Secret Intelligence Service."[45]

Natalya comes along and asks him about his relationship with Trevelyan: "He was your friend. And now he's your enemy and you are going to kill him. It is that simple?" Bond assents, to what Natalya protests, telling him she's not impressed with the nature of his violent job and his idea of heroism: "All the heroes I know are dead". Natalya then asks: "How can you act like this?! How can you be so cold?!" and, defining the lone-wolf essence of James Bond that harkens back to the pages of Ian Fleming, he simply replies: "That's what keeps me alive". In Gardner's book, Bond gives her a more realistic, somewhat tender and educative description: "I do a necessary job. If I didn't do it, someone else would. I simply have to level things off so that one day there will be some true kind of peace in the world."[46] Therefore, Natalya is the perfect example of how to shape an attractive woman meant to please Bond and the audience into an integral part of the story, as a character with the scientific knowledge to foil the enemy plan and a way to help the audience to get inside Bond's feelings and insecurities, something Pierce Brosnan always wanted to give to his James Bond portrayal.

Another interesting aspect of Natalya Simonova is the fact that she was the first Bond girl to have a lengthy action scene without Bond's involvement and, notably, long before Bond meets her: as the GoldenEye weapon targets the Severnaya Space Weapon Centre where she works in, Natalya escapes from exploding computers, pipes blowing away, and even a MiG plane crashing into the structure. Actress Izabella Scorupco remembered her role in an interview with *ActionAdventure* in 2004: "I thought my Bond girl was just really human, a very human being in a Bond movie because she was this Russian computer nerd. I never looked really smashing. I had one outfit throughout the whole movie. Did I ever wear high heels in the movie? I didn't."[47]

The dark side of the *GoldenEye* women is Xenia Onatopp, played by Famke Janssen. If Natalya was brave but at the same time innocent, conservative and discreet-looking, Xenia is her exact opposite: bold, sexual, dangerous and decidedly evil. She is, out of all the women of the film, the closest to a female version of Bond, just that she stands on the other side: she enjoys a high-stakes baccarat game, a dangerous race through the mountains, and also likes to drink a vodka martini ("Straight up, with a twist", she suggestively has it prepared). Xenia has a military background, like Bond, and says double-entendres on occasions. In contrast with Natalya's modest-looking wardrobe, she wears tight black outfits and designer dresses with a pronounced neckline. Chances are that if Xenia and Bond were on the same side, they would make a perfect duo. But of course, she's not and, though she has some time to enjoy Bond in a perverse sexual game in a spa, she never neglects her duty of killing him by doing her trademark move of crushing him with her tighs, with Bond ultimately defeating her in her own game. In the words of Famke Janssen: "Xenia comes very close (to Bond): she loves to drive fast, shoot guns, gamble… and she loves men – in her own way. There's a kind of animal attraction between her and James because Xenia's definitely an animal."[48]

Among the long list of Bond vixens, Xenia Onatopp combines the evilness of Fiona Volpe from *Thunderball* with the background of Anya Amasova in *The Spy Who Loved Me*, only to be less human and more of a cold machine that provides, at the same time, sex and death. If Natalya was the first Bond girl to have an action scene made specifically for her, Xenia became the one who gave the saga the first explicit sex scene, albeit not with 007 but with the ill-fated Admiral Chuck Farrell played by *Never Say Never Again* actor Billy Mitchell, whom she kills with her tights in order to steal the Tiger helicopter.

We know little about the background of these two leading female characters of the film, but we can have an idea on Xenia's past coming from Famke Janssen herself while describing her character's feisty nature: "She has grown up in Russia, with shortages and little money. So she's like a child in a sweet shop, with a bag full of gold coins"[49]. At the same time, author John Gardner indicates that she worked as a pilot for the KGB "for a year, just before the '91 coup"[50].

We do know a little more of Natalya's past, especially of her education in conservative Soviet Russia, thanks to the novelization, where it is revealed that their parents would be horrified at the way she made love to Bond: "In the distance, she seemed to hear her mother, flustered, *Natalya have you no shame* when, years ago, she had caught her with a local boy"[51]. She also had a very caring family, which "had gone without a number of luxuries"[52] to buy her a watch before she entered university. In concordance with Gardner's novelization, Izabella Scorupco observed that Natalya's childhood probably was very much similar to her own: "I was born in Poland during the Cold War and know of the hardship and oppression first hand. (…) When I was a youngster in Poland I had to cope with the fact that my mother, a doctor, underwent interrogation for three days after treating someone who had a political bias."[53]

Before his encounters with Natalya and Xenia, 007 first interacts with Caroline, the MI6 psychological advisor who has been sent to Monaco to evaluate him. She is, actually, the first woman to yell at him for his reckless actions –driving his old Aston Martin DB5 at top speed on a mountain road– which goes worse and worse as Xenia Onatopp appears with her red Ferrari and challenges him for a race, in a scene that five years later inspired John Woo's *Mission: Impossible II*. Bond disregards every one of Caroline's comments: "We're having a pleasant drive in the country and you have to bring psychology into it." Eventually, he wins the race and decides to consider Caroline's commands. As he stops the car, she becomes what is perhaps Bond's easiest "conquest" in the film: revealing a chilled bottle of Bollinger '88 on the glove compartment of his Aston Martin, Bond jokingly comments: "As you can see, I have no problem with a female authority". The woman, at first panicked at Bond's irresponsible actions, falls to his charms and allows Bond to kiss her.

Closer to the half of the story, agent 007 visits the British Secret Service, where he finds a familiar face: Miss Moneypenny, this time played by Samantha Bond. The character, established by the Ian Fleming novels, occasionally flirted with James Bond and was openly attracted to him, particularly in the films where it was remarkably portrayed by Lois Maxwell for 23 years and 14 films –with Sean Connery, George Lazenby and Roger Moore– and Caroline Bliss in the two Timothy Dalton entries.

While Samantha Bond's Moneypenny has represented more or less the same traits of the character in her other three Bond films (*Tomorrow Never Dies*, *The World Is Not Enough* and *Die Another Day*), in *GoldenEye* she tries to be a light symbol of female liberation: she disregards Bond's comments about her looks, tells him she has a date with a gentleman and considers his usual flirting as "sexual harassment". Much harsher, though, is the new female M played by Judi Dench for the first time in 17 years.

Author Iain Johnston narrates how M became a woman after a suggestion Martin Campbell made to screenwriter Bruce Feirstein: "At 6 o'clock one morning, just before shooting, he gave an early draft to Feirstein and asked: 'What do you think of the M scene?' The American replied: 'It's a bunch of white guys sitting around talking.' So Campbell suggested: 'Well, why don't you try it as a woman?' By 11 a.m. M had changed sex"[54]. This twist would fit the current times, considering the choice of Stella Rimmington as the Director of the real-life MI5 ("They certainly look very similar", noted Prime Minister John Major[55]), the section of the British Intelligence dedicated to the investigation of threats coming from the United Kingdom. In both the Ian Fleming novels and the early Bond films, the director of MI6 was a Royal Navy Admiral played by Bernard Lee and Robert Brown. The tense encounter between Bond and Judi Dench's M would be the first chapter of a very discreet and loose story arc in the series that would follow into the Daniel Craig era, reaching an end with 2012's *Skyfall*, where Dench's M dies after a shootout held on a Scottish lodge.

Summoning him to her office, M notes that Bond disregards her, considering her not capable of running the department: "You think I'm a counter. A bean counter more interested in my numbers than your instincts". Then, she begins to discipline him with a few severe words: "I think you are a sexist, misogynist dinosaur. A relic of the Cold War, whose boyish charms, though wasted on me, obviously appealed to that young woman I sent out to evaluate you." Then, she continues with a more rational approach, to which Bond feels more comfortable: "If you think for a moment I don't have the balls to send a man out to die, your instincts are dead wrong. I've no compunction about sending you to your death. But I won't do it on a whim, even with your cavalier attitude towards life."

It is, at this point, when Bond begins to warm to the new M and understands she has the courage of her predecessor, that she's into the life and death philosophy that concerns the job of a field operative, as evidenced by the novelization: "Bond had no reply to this impassioned speech. If anything, he did have a tad more respect for the new M"[56]. A literary masterstroke that reflects their mutual understanding comes as he leaves the office and M stops him. As he turns around, she says: "Come back alive."

While Judi Dench played two versions of M for the Pierce Brosnan and Daniel Craig portrayals, with different backgrounds, the character is somehow maternal to Bond, as he becomes a man of her confidence and is regarded as "the best (agent) she has" in *The World Is Not Enough*. With each passing film, her screen time got bigger and bigger (*GoldenEye* is, in fact, her shortest appearance in the series). Something similar takes place during the Daniel Craig movies, although the covert mother-son connection is much more stressed, particularly in *Skyfall*, her last Bond film. Ralph Fiennes replaced her as M (Lt. Colonel Gareth Mallory) after she dies in the very last minutes of the 2012 film, but a posthumous message from her is the catalyst for the main action of 2015's *SPECTRE*.

The only *GoldenEye* girl who has no interaction with James Bond is a small female part played by Minnie Driver: Irina, the mistress of arms dealer Valentin Zukovsky. She is there to deliver one of the funniest scenes of the film as she horrendously tries to sing Tammy Wynette's "Stand By Your Man" in Zukovsky's empty nightclub. Bond thinks her performance is reminiscent to a strangled cat and Zukovsky, preferring to have his chat with Bond undisturbed, sends her to "take a hike".

Despite the ridiculous nature of this character, Driver has shown a lot of gratitude to the role. Before she accepted the role, she was very short of money and living in Uruguay. "I literally had five bucks to my name and I'm in the bikini that I'd lived in for the last three months," she confessed on NBC's *Today* in 2018. After receiving the call from her agent, she was unsure to accept the role fearing her Bond girl image would ruin her professional career, but her agent convinced her: "Are you crazy?! You are not going to kill anybody or sleep with anybody, get on the plane!" [57] Two years after *GoldenEye*, Driver became popular with her role in *Good Will Hunting*, earning an Oscar nomination. In 2017, she was reunited with

Pierce Brosnan in *Spinning Man*, where she played Guy Pearce's wife, a prominent role in the film.

Courageous, wild, provocative, independent, strong, determined. The women of *GoldenEye* were the among first to psychologically question James Bond's lifestyle and manners, allowing some brief moments of self-analysis in the character never before seen since the days of Ian Fleming's novels. At the same time, they were seductive and courageous enough to be a relevant and very interesting part of the story. With *GoldenEye*, gone were the days where what mattered most were only the looks, and the personality of Bond girls —and their interactions with Bond— also became as equally as important.

GOLDENEYE AND BETRAYAL

Betrayal is perhaps the most important subject in *GoldenEye*. The characters, from the beginning to the end of the movie (and even *before* the events of the movie) are linked to each other through a minefield of treachery that harkens back to the end of World War II.

The most notorious case of betrayal in *GoldenEye* is, of course, the one from Alec Trevelyan to Great Britain: former British agent 006, a comrade fallen in the field of honour, now turned into Janus: Britain's number one enemy. He is plotting revenge against the country and to James Bond, who placed the success of the mission above the life of his fellow agent and friend, as he carried on with the objective of blowing up the Arkangel facility and escaped as Trevelyan was gunned down by Ourumov. The former 006, however, sees betrayal the other way around. This harkens back to 1945 when the Lienz Cossacks were betrayed by British officers, surrendered to Stalin and promptly executed or, in the case of Trevelyan's parents (who belonged to this group), forced by the situation to commit suicide. Janus wants to make England learn the cost of their betrayal with another betrayal – the one of its adopted "son" since MI6 thought he wouldn't remember his origins due to his early age.

The web of betrayal keeps extending: the Lienz Cossacks have previously betrayed the Russians and joined the Nazi troops to fight the

Red Army. This fact is evoked by Bond to Ourumov after infiltrating Trevelyan's ICBM hideout train, where the General has Natalya at gunpoint: "You knew, didn't you? He's a Lienz Cossack. He'll betray you! Just like everyone else". Even if it turns out to be a strategic move by Bond to distract General Ourumov, he tries to underline the fact that Trevelyan is, plain and simple, a traitor. He's not a son of Mother Russia as Ourumov is or a true believer of the communist cause. He comes from a family that has betrayed Russia and he himself is a traitor to England so he could double-cross Ourumov in a future as he did with "everyone else".

The other betrayal, for Trevelyan, comes from James Bond himself when "his loyalty went to the mission" instead of his friend. Bond reset the timers to three minutes instead of the planned six and complicated Trevelyan's escape after getting "shot" by Ourumov in 1986. The result: half of his face is now a mass of burn scars, the reason why he identifies himself with the Roman god, Janus.

According to Roman mythology, Janus has two faces: one looking at the past, the other looking at the future. He symbolizes the time, the transition between past and future[58], a fact that the film embodies perfectly story-wise: Alec Trevelyan's plan consists of a tough financial future for England by judging the country for what it did in the past, particularly to the Lienz Cossacks. However, Trevelyan also attributes his new alias to Bond's doing: "It wasn't God who gave me this face. It was you, setting the timers for three minutes instead of six."

The professional rivalry between Alec Trevelyan and James Bond, represented in the 00 section by the numbers 006 and 007, is also comprised inside this great subject of betrayal the film deals with. Not in vain during the fight in the climax Trevelyan tells Bond, held at gunpoint, that "he was always better".

There even is a biblical approach to the rivalry between the two: according to the Bible, number six is associated with the evils of Satan, the manifestation of sin and human weakness. The combination of three sixes represents the Beast of Revelation[59]. On the other hand, number seven is related to completeness and physical and spiritual perfection, the foundation of God's word[60]. Trevelyan (006) bears one of the numbers of the diabolical beast; he represents sin and treachery while Bond (007) represents what is perfect and incorruptible. The same applies in the physical appearance of both men, as one of them has a side of his face burned and the other appears to be a perfectly-looking human being. Trevelyan knows Bond's "fatal weakness" (the attraction towards women) and captures Natalya to place him in a situation similar to the Archangel mission: killing him and saving the world but compromising Natalya's life, or losing time in shooting Ourumov (who is holding Natalya at gunpoint) and allow Trevelyan an easy way out. Previously, he also tries to possess the woman romantically tied with his former friend: "James and I shared everything… absolutely everything. To the victor go the spoils", he explains as he slowly begins to stroke her face, trying to kiss her. *Thou shalt not covet thy neighbour's wife…*

Deep inside, Trevelyan feels begrudged both for Bond and for England. At the same time, Bond is also struck by the fact a friend has betrayed both him and the Realm. This is evidenced in the very last minutes, as the two are having a final hand-to-hand showdown in a very small platform at the bottom of the antenna, unprotected to a 650-feet drop: "For England, James?" questions Trevelyan. "No, for me", Bond coldly replies as he lets his old friend fall to his death.

The subject of treachery still plays an important part in the relationship between other characters like Natalya Simonova and Boris Grishenko, a computer hacker employed by Janus. They both work in the Severnaya installation and they were friends, but Boris ends up betraying Natalya twice. The first is during the incident taking place in the scene where we are first introduced to them, both computer programmers in the Space Weapon Control Centre, an installation located in the loneliness of the Siberian plateau. Due to his advanced knowledge in systems, Boris makes a deal with General Ourumov to become the one "survivor" to the GoldenEye blast. Of course, Ourumov and his accomplice Xenia Onatopp ignored the fact that Natalya was hidden and survived both their attack and the destruction of Severnaya, becoming a very uncomfortable loose end. Escaping from the wreckage, she managed to go to St. Petersburg where, unbeknownst of Boris' league with the aggressors, gets to contact him via e-mail and arrange an encounter at the Our Lady of Smolensk church. As they both meet, the deceitful Boris hands her into Xenia.

Investigating Ourumov and his implication on the Severnaya affair, M comments James Bond that the General "doesn't fit the profile of a traitor" according to the analysts. However, Bond knows him better and mistrusts these observations. Ourumov is, indeed, a traitor to Mother Russia – or, at least, to *modern* Russia. His dossier points out the highlights of his military and political résumé:

> "Rehabilitated by Gorbachev in 1987, following the destruction of the Arkangel facility (…) In spite of being given command of Space Division by Gorbachev, Ourumov is believed to have been behind the Gorbachev coup but the inquiry was dropped after the suicide of a co-conspirator"

The most notable aspect in this brief paragraph of the electronic dossier briefly shown on a TV screen behind M's desk is that the General appears to have betrayed none other than Mikhail Gorbachev, leader of the Soviet Union until its demise in 1991. Although nothing is specified in the film, script or novelization of *GoldenEye*, it's not too difficult to see that a fervent communist and lover of the cause as Ourumov would have disagreed with Gorbachev's *glasnost* and *perestroika* policies which made the USSR friendlier to the world.

The *Avgustovskiy Putch* or August Coup of 1991 consisted of a state of emergency declared by Vice-president Gennady Yanayev and other conservative members of the Soviet government, the army and the KGB. The committee was formed while Gorbachev was vacationing on his dacha in Crimea, under the pretext that he was unable to exercise the presidency. Their main objective was to avoid the approval of the New Union Treaty, which would reorganize the USSR in a more federative and less centralized country, and would eventually lead to the dissolution of the Soviet Union.

This emergency state committee banned every newspaper in Moscow, except for nine which were controlled by the Communist Party. On August 19, 1991, armoured vehicles and tanks rolled into the Russian capital as citizens erected barricades against the Soviet army and their vehicles. Boris Yeltsin, President of the Russian Federation, confronted the committee, calling their actions an anti-constitutional coup. Some of the insurgent forces ordered an attack against the White House (Russian Parliament), made effective as August 21 began, and culminating with the accidental death of three young civilians. These casualties brought the coup attempt to a halt. Gorbachev returned from Crimea and clarified that he wasn't suffering from poor health as Yanayev claimed, calling the state of emergency an unconstitutional manoeuvre against his authority. These events led to Gorbachev's resignation, the ban of the Communist Party and the definitive dissolution of the Soviet Union, with a now very popular Yeltsin established as the President of the Russian Federation.

Most of the conspirators against Gorbachev were arrested and tried between 1992 and 1994. Three of the members, Boris Pugo (Minister of Interior), Nikolay Kruchina (Administrator of Affairs of the Central Committee), and Sergey Akhromeyev (Gorbachev's Military Advisor) committed suicide. It is understood that Ourumov was linked to one of these men, and their suicide dropped any lead of his involvement in the coup[61].

Still in command of the Space Division of the Russian Army, Ourumov is now a reluctant member of Boris Yeltsin's government in 1995, under the watch of Yelstin's (fictional) Minister of Defence, Dimitri Mishkin. Mishkin is the exact opposite of what Ourumov is: civilian, democratic, bureaucratic and part of the young new generation of politicians brought after the dissolution of the USSR.

Given full access and authority to the Severnaya station, as the Head of the Space Division, General Ourumov arrives with the stolen EMP-resistant Tiger helicopter to the place, accompanied by Xenia Onatopp, a Russian Army Colonel. The surprised Duty Officer is told that this is an unscheduled test of the defence systems – a war simulation. Right after the officer hands the General the authorization codes and the key to arm the GoldenEye weapon, he is gunned down by Onatopp along with the other military and civilian employees except for Boris (who "escaped" before they arrived) and Natalya, hidden in the kitchen. Both the General and the Colonel set Severnaya as the target and escape before the station is blown to bits with Natalya surviving by the skin of her teeth.

To regain power and become "the next Iron Man of Russia" (as he sees himself), Ourumov forged an alliance with the Janus Syndicate. He wants to take over Russia again and bring the old order back, as his collaborators tried to do with Gorbachev, which resulted in the definitive termination of the Soviet Union. With Janus on his side, he will collect a big sum of money, hit the financial heart of Great Britain and be powerful enough to (probably) throw Yelstin and his bunch of civilian guys out in replacement for a Communist and military government, perhaps led by himself. The plan, of course, requires the assassination of innocent sons of Mother Russia to achieve completion and he doesn't even flinch at the prospect of betraying his country because, now, he surely sees his country as "infiltrated" by a wave of capitalists.

Minister Mishkin and the council later inquiry General Ourumov at the Winter Palace in St. Petersburg, regarding the Severnaya incident taking place three days earlier. Showing a notable contempt to civilians involved in his area, the General arrives ten minutes later to the meeting. Author John Gardner describes the scene in the film's novelization: "Mishkin was undeniably annoyed. Pacing the huge room with its baroque ceiling and high windows (…) and constantly looking at his watch. As a rule, even senior officers did not keep the Minister of Defence waiting"[62].

Ourumov arrives and delivers his report, concluding that the crime was "committed by Siberian Separatists seeking to create political unrest" and then presents his resignation. As the council rejects his idea, the Minister tells him all they need is the assurance that there are no other GoldenEye satellites. The General, confidently, assures him that. But he's dumbstruck when Mishkin asks him about the *two* missing technicians: he only knew about Boris Grishenko because he was the insider, the one they rigged to "survive". The Minister brings to Ourumov's attention that the body of Natalya Fyodorovna Simonova, a programmer, wasn't found among the dead. Now, the politician has spotted a weak point of the General, and he doesn't hesitate to defy him: "It would seem presumptuous to blame this incident on Siberian Separatists before the whereabouts of your own people are determined."

Ourumov's guilt is confirmed to Mishkin when Natalya Simonova, captured with James Bond as they are both framed for the Severnaya incident, accuses the General: "He killed everyone and stole the GoldenEye". The Minister remains fairly undisturbed until Natalya declares there was another satellite, invalidating the "assurance" Ourumov gave him at the Winter Palace that there wasn't. Seconds later, the General burst in the room and overrules him of the investigation, claiming it was his: "You are out of order!" he barks. Confident of his authority, Mishkin replies: "From what I've heard, it is *you* who is out of order." Ourumov answers by picking up Bond's handgun, lying over the table of the interrogation room: "I've seen this gun in the hand of the enemy. Do you even know who the enemy is?" To Ourumov, Bond is an enemy of the country who should be defeated no matter what, or that is at least what he tries to imply to the Minister: that they are both on the same boat, fighting the foreigner, the British capitalist agent. But to the Defence Minister, this is an old story, this is a new Russia and he's now more than convinced of Ourumov's treachery. He calls a guard to arrest the General, who quickly reacts by shooting both the soldier and Mishkin at point blank.

Betrayal is a primary subject of *GoldenEye* and is also the web that links all the events of the film, from the historical aspects to the great chases, action scenes and stunts. Future James Bond films, like *The World, Is Not Enough*, *Die Another Day* and *Casino Royale* would also deal with the issues of loyalty, trust and betrayal, but *GoldenEye* did it in an iconic and philosophical way not regularly seen in the series.

GOLDENEYE
AND ITS GENERATION

With the release of *GoldenEye*, a new generation of James Bond fans emerged in 1995. Most of them were born between the second half of the 1980s and the first half of the 1990s, with ages between eight or ten when the film was first screened in their local cinema, released on home video or broadcasted on TV for the first time. At the same time, film series like *Die Hard* and *Lethal Weapon*, initiated in the late '80s and continued well into the '90s, replicated somehow that Bond school of action heroes that had a sense of humour from time to time. These heroes were played by actors like Bruce Willis, Mel Gibson and Arnold Schwarzenegger, who had his very own Bond imitation in 1994 with *True Lies*. Not far from them, Tom Clancy's CIA analyst Jack Ryan –played by Alec Baldwin and Harrison Ford– was the leading character in films like *The Hunt For Red October, Patriot Games* and *Clear And Present Danger* and was often described as a "James Bond for the '90s"[63].

These movies, now considered classics of the action genre, entertained an entire childhood through escapism, fun and spectacular action sequences, comprised of explosive chases and hair-raising stunts. While they were strong contenders for a James Bond that was set to return in this decade, the production team of *GoldenEye* diminished the competition. Director Martin Campbell observed that these action heroes were "blue-collar heroes and just do not have the sophistication or style of Bond"[64], while production designer Peter Lamont, who worked in *True Lies*, shifted the critics comparison between Schwarzenegger's Harry Tasker and 007: "(He) had a wife bored out of her skull and an out-of-control daughter. That was not James Bond"[65].

Even though James Bond was different from these "blue-collar" heroes, their success and phenomenon had to be considered by the filmmakers if they wanted to ensure James Bond's relevance in the 1990s. It was important to contemplate that the Bond films had to be modernized to compete with those heroes out there and, at the same time, provide a window for more traditional audiences who were after the visual glamour and style which has historically made the James Bond films unique. "I watched all sixteen Bond films on tape, just to remind myself what was good about them. The humour and action and romantic quality were there, to be developed and exploited in this seventeenth picture," reflected Campbell in 1995, as he promised to "deliver a Bond just as classy, just as romantic, but hopefully even more unbeatable than the others"[66].

The insurgence of political correctness played a small part in the production of the film, given that critics and audiences often wondered if some of Bond's attitudes would fit into the new social climate of the 1990s. In hindsight, the feuds about political correctness in those days were much lighter when compared to, for example, the late 2010s: the emergence of social movements like #MeToo has carried the discussion to a whole new ground where movies or their actors are regularly boycotted online, with their careers sometimes destroyed. But the truth is that the character changed little and remained more or less the same Bond, only with very slight twists to be in tune with the times. Both the protagonist and the director insisted that keeping the essence of 007 was crucial for the film's success. Martin Campbell noted that Bond "is still as sexist as he ever was. Cancelling out his chauvinism would be a mistake. He must remain a womanizer. The only thing he doesn't do anymore is smoke."[67] Pierce Brosnan went further than Campbell's thoughts on the conversation with authors Lee Pfeiffer and Phillip Lisa for the book *The Incredible World of 007*: "I find the whole political correctness thing to be a certain form of censorship. I find it very boring and tiring, especially when it comes down to a piece of entertainment such as Bond. For example, take the part of Xenia (…) Bond deals with her in his own way. She's messed with him and he'll mess with her. That's what turned people on in the first place. It's part of the mystique."[68]

Instead of transforming Bond's persona or submit him to a radical change influenced by political correctness, *GoldenEye* makes slight concessions to political correctness via female characters like Natalya Simonova, who regularly treats him in a dominant way: "Don't stand there! Get us out of here!" she complains, to what Bond sarcastically replies "Yes, sir"; and the female M, who directly calls him a "sexist, misogynist dinosaur" pointing out his macho antics and his "cavalier attitude towards life". This sort of flippant acknowledge skimming the comical territory proved to be a much better approach than offering a subdued and lukewarm version of James Bond, and shaped the mould of the character for the rest of the decade.

GoldenEye is firmly set into the 1990s, and it could be said that the film is "dated", but in the good sense of the word: the stunts, the action, the characters and the historical background all contrive to create an ambient that places this thriller in the podium of the most prominent action classics of the decade – a list that includes *Die Hard 2*, *True Lies*, *Mission: Impossible* and *Speed*, to name a few. The movie followed the recipe and structure of these productions: the big stunts, action, shootouts and humour that made them rewatchable for countless times, but with the distinction of Bond's unique mannerisms, style and globe-trotting adventures which were pretty much absent from these rival films. Comparing *GoldenEye* with other rival productions of the decade, author James Chapman points out that the colourful cinematography of the film was probably meant "as a form of differentiation, as the tendency in most other action thrillers of the 1990s (…) had been towards a grainier, grittier look in which much of the action is under-lit."[69] The result is attractive for both the classic Bond fan as well as the newcomer Bond fan, as previously exposed.

The passion and enthusiasm coming from these fans can be attributed to the huge merchandising produced for young audiences and tied into the movie. The publicity machine aimed to attract some infants to the new Bond, as evidenced by the production of toys like cap-firing replicas of silenced Walther PPK handguns and Corgi's famous reproductions of the films vehicles like Bond's Aston Martin DB5 and BMW Z3, or Xenia's

Ferrari F355. "It was very much a return to form compared to the rather underwhelming collectables produced for the previous film, *Licence To Kill*. In some ways it was reminiscent of the 1960s with all types of memorabilia produced for a wide demographic, from toys gun sets, model cars, trading card albums and hand-held computer games aimed at kids, to razors, pens and special bottles of Smirnoff vodka for adults," reflects Reuben Wakeman, a huge 007 collector and the man behind the website *Toys of Bond*. "There was a strong push with many commercial partners to market the film too, with various types of promotional packaging, shop and retail displays for products ranging from Terry's Chocolate in the UK, Perrier in France, Shreddies cereal in Canada, Pepsi in Singapore, Varta batteries and even *GoldenEye* peanuts in the Netherlands, to name just a few. In fact in the autumn of 1995 *GoldenEye* seemed to be pretty much everywhere, you could even collect tokens from special tins of tuna in the UK to claim a *GoldenEye* lunchbox!"

Following a long-gone tradition shared by earlier James Bond films like *Dr No*, *For Your Eyes Only*, *A View To A Kill* and *Licence To Kill*, Topps also released an official *GoldenEye* comic adaptation, whose first issue was released on January 1996 and unexpectedly discontinued. Despite the good-looking drawings by Rick Magyar and the clever script adaptation by Don McGregor, who has previously worked on original Bond comics, issues two and three never saw the light. McGregor explained the reasons to Matt Sherman on an interview with *Collecting 007* magazine in 2000: "The day the entire book of the three Bond issues, completely drawn, completely inked, completely lettered, was placed in my hands, was also the day I was informed that the book would never see print. (...) To make things worse, it wasn't even the sales that killed us. Sales weren't spectacular, but they were good. (...) There were problems with licensing. Jim Salicrup, who had championed getting Bond done as comics (...) had to make the decision not to print because he hadn't received necessary approvals from all the parties concerned, and we were now months away from the release of the movie."[70]

But without the shadow of a doubt, the most successful *GoldenEye*-related toy would come two years after the film, in 1997, with a video game made for Nintendo. The success of both *GoldenEye* the film and the game attracted a bigger and faithful Bond audience for films like *Tomorrow Never Dies*, *The World Is Not Enough* and *Die Another Day*, all with Pierce Brosnan's leading portrayal. The reboot of the series in 2006 with the adaptation of *Casino Royale* distanced some of them from James Bond, who didn't embrace Daniel Craig's grittier and emotional performance which continued in films like *Quantum of Solace*, *Skyfall*, *SPECTRE* as well as the upcoming Bond 25, set for April 2020.

Part of this generation is composer Yannick Zenhäusern, who has frequently named *GoldenEye* as not only his favourite James Bond movie but as his favourite movie of all time. A proud defender of Eric Serra's score for the film and an integral part of the team behind *GoldenEye: Source* and *GoldenEye 25*, two fan video game projects, Zenhäusern thinks that EON Productions is trying to keep Bond alive with each passing film and up to date, but that he thinks *Die Another Day* "was the last real Bond movie". He claims to have watched all the Daniel Craig Bond films, but he isn't clearly too fond of them: "I couldn't possibly pick a favourite cause I really don't like any of them, sorry. Where have all the iconic elements gone?"

Other members of this so-called "*GoldenEye* Generation" are much more sympathetic to the current James Bond era initiated in 2006, or – actually– on 14 October 2005 when Daniel Craig was unveiled as the sixth Bond actor in London. Benjamin Lind, who runs *The Bond Bulletin*, was 14 when he first saw *GoldenEye* in the big screen early in 1996. He refuses to call it his favourite ("every film has certain highlights as well as drawbacks and I treasure every one of them") but *GoldenEye* was his first Bond experience and the one who made him become an expert on the subject and cultivate a great love for the franchise, which he expressed on his 2016 documentary *A Bond For Life*. On the new wave of James Bond films, Lind was unsure about Daniel Craig's casting, but he quickly changed his mind when he saw *Casino Royale*: "I was relieved when many in the audience stood up and applauded when Craig walked towards the camera in the main title sequence. This was a signature moment and I knew he would have a good tenure as 007."[71] A similar opinion is shared by Austin Skinner, contributor of the Trevelyan's Mainframe column in *The GoldenEye Dossier*: "I do love where Craig has taken Agent 007. With the borderline redundancy of personal vendettas that have plagued his era, Craig has been able to stay compelling and fresh with each of his outings as Bond. (...) My favourites within his catalogue are *Casino Royale* and *Skyfall*."[72]

As for the James Bond films prior to *GoldenEye*, Zenhäusern shows some favouritism to the ones of the Roger Moore era: "I just love to have a chuckle every now and then. The scores were mostly very brilliant and some very fine Bond girls". This is also partially shared by Skinner, who names *The Man With The Golden Gun* among his most liked Bond films along with *On Her Majesty's Secret Service* and *Thunderball*, starring George Lazenby and Sean Connery. Lind, on the other hand, is keener on *The Living Daylights*, Timothy Dalton's 007 debut, particularly for John Barry's soundtrack and the locations in Austria. Taking into account the aforementioned movies, it can be assumed that this *GoldenEye* generation has a penchant for movies with grandiose action sequences, beautiful women, eye-popping locales and some humour over a darker and grittier Bond film – which does not rules out the presence of a psychologically conflicted Bond from time to time, something which was even present in *GoldenEye*, as the secret agent ponders his confrontation with Alec Trevelyan while relaxing with Natalya on a Cuban beach.

When talking about this *GoldenEye* generation, a special mention has to be made to Kimberly Last, who in December 1994 created the first ever James Bond-related website. Today many pages abound on the subject and fans get updates of people following the steps of agent 007 through official and unofficial sites and Twitter accounts, however, in the 1990s, Last's site was the biggest resources for Bond news and the first hit on the search engines of those times, like *Yahoo!* and *Altavista*. She remembers the release of *GoldenEye* as "a huge event" and points out that "everyone was excited. Some people did not like Pierce because of *Remington Steele*, they thought he was wimpy. But I don't remember people being negative before it came out."

The generational aspect of the film plays a good part in the adoration by these people, since it made many concessions to everyone who was at a very early age in the 1990s: it's the film for those who grew up with the slow Internet connections, marvelled with the prospect of e-mails and another kind of technologies: the technologies that, back then –and opposed to these days–, were only used by their parents and that the kids could only touch with the appropriate permission.

In 2006's *Casino Royale*, we see James Bond hacking into M's secure website, something he needed Natalya Simonova for in *GoldenEye* to prevent Trevelyan's retaliation against England to succeed. The prospect of the Internet being a novelty and a potentially dangerous weapon also dates the film in 1995, a year where movies like *Hackers* and *The Net* used the World Wide Web as a key aspect of their plots. Unlike future Bond adventures dealing with these technologies, by the mid-1990s Internet was represented as a tool that very few people or experts could handle properly, and that the man of the street was beginning to familiarize with. The times when buying a PC for domestic use was something few people could afford. Let alone the idea of "hacking" a web site, an attack Boris does for fun against the US Department of Justice – something that is not unusual to see nowadays in action films or political thrillers, or even in real life. The James Bond bosses themselves were collateral victims of an electronic correspondence hacking to Sony Pictures by the end of 2014, which resulted in the leak of two preliminary scripts of the upcoming *SPECTRE*.

The 1990s was also a decade marked by the evolution of communications and media, a subject which is, in fact, thoroughly exploited on Pierce Brosnan's second 007 outing *Tomorrow Never Dies*. However, there is also an interesting dialogue between M and James Bond that should deserve special attention, generational-wise. The secret agent inquires if the satellite pictures showing the Severnaya installation are live, to what M replies: "Unlike the American government, we prefer not to get our bad news from *CNN*." This refers, of course, to the popular American news channel *Cable News Network* founded by Ted Turner in 1980, the first to provide news 24 hours a day, whose popularity skyrocketed in 1991 due to their rather dramatic and intense coverage of the Gulf War.

Communication studies and essays also refer to a certain "CNN effect", which has been explored, among others, by Professor Eytan Gilboa from the Harvard University. This so-called CNN effect considers the notion of 24/7 real-time coverage of political events or wars accelerating the pace of international communications, as well as forcing leaders to take immediate action on certain subjects that they probably wouldn't have been previously interested in, leading them to act in no time and bypassing the chance to at least consider different options due to the intense media pressure[73]. Perhaps what Judi Dench's character tried to mean is that the British government, or at least its intelligence service, is ready to take action even before they feel this media pressure, unlike their American counterparts. In the end, it's just a barely noticeable playful line, but it's another thing that acknowledges the notable influence of telecommunications in the taking of big political decisions in the 1990s, where the film firmly takes place. Again, the effect of mass media and wars would be a central aspect of *Tomorrow Never Dies*, but in a slight way, *GoldenEye* paved the road for it and set the viewers firmly in the present day.

Another detail that attaches *GoldenEye* to the 1990s is the costumes, particularly when it comes to James Bond's clothing. This was the first of five consecutive Bond films where Lindy Hemming worked as a costume designer. While in the Ian Fleming novels, set in the 1950s, the literary Bond dressed with minimalistic-looking clothes, mostly with an "old dark blue tropical worsted suit, a sleeveless white cotton shirt and a black knitted tie"[74]; the sartorial tastes for the cinematic Bond have been updated to different styles fashion-wise, as evidenced by the Roger Moore films where the suits by Cyril Castle and Angelo Roma adopted much of the 1970s fashion, with lapels and tie knots becoming wider and bigger.

The wardrobe for Pierce Brosnan in *GoldenEye*, made by Brioni in Italy, included a grey suit with box cover check, a Prince of Wales check suit and a navy Birdseye suit, paired with woven silk ties from Sulka, in blue with mostly yellow and red details[75]. Hemming intended to evoke the look of Sean Connery, dressed by Saville Row in the first film of the series while making the suits very contemporary to the times.

"The *GoldenEye* suits have a number of elements that make them trendy for the 1990s," notes Matt Spaiser, author of the website *The Suits of James Bond*. "The most obvious is the button-three front that most of the suits have, which was very popular at the time. James Bond had occasionally worn button three suits in the past, but he was usually a two-button man. Suit jackets have a full cut, large shoulders and a longer length, and the trousers are wide-legged with pleats, all contributing to the 1990s look." A New York-based graphic designer and fashion expert, Spaiser also pointed out that, although they were made in Italy, the suits Bond wears in *GoldenEye* were made of English cloths. "The suits are also detailed with hacking pockets, ticket pockets and double vents to give them a connection to England. Brioni's Roman cut is actually inspired by the Savile Row military cut, making them a distant cousin of Bond's former English suits."

Something that makes a movie generational is, without doubt, the music. There are many examples of James Bond soundtrack albums that were a product of their times: while John Barry made music for 007 between the 1960s and the late 1980s, composers like Marvin Hamlisch and Bill Conti used the disco influence in films like *The Spy Who Loved Me* and *For Your Eyes Only*, released in 1977 and 1981, while popular bands like Duran Duran, A-ha and The Pretenders made vocal versions for the Bond films in the second half of the 1980s. The use of popular singers to sing along the main title sequence of a 007 film has drawn Adele and Sam Smith fans to the theatre to watch *Skyfall* and *SPECTRE* just to listen to their idols' song featured in the movie in the same way some The Beatles fans adore *Live And Let Die* for Paul McCartney's title theme tune in 1973.

In the case of *GoldenEye*, the score was composed by Eric Serra and the main title tune performed by Tina Turner and written by U2's Bono and The Edge, all very popular names in the 1990s. The theme achieved great success and reached a Top 5 hit on many European countries, while many Bond fans were also pleased with Turner's voice which brought back memories of the old Shirley Bassey themes for the series. On the other hand, Serra's soundtrack was less traditional and is perhaps the most atypical of the James Bond soundtracks. True to his style, the French composer offered an electronic and industrial sound for *GoldenEye* in the vein of his score for *Léon: The Professional* released one year earlier. In fact, the melody for *GoldenEye*'s end title song, "The Experience of Love" (also performed by Serra) is lifted straight from a track from the 1994 film, "The Game is Over", heard among the very last scenes of the Luc Besson movie.

"When *GoldenEye* opened in the theatres, Serra's score thrilled his fans and even sold well to a younger listening audience in record stores. To the mass of long-time Bond fans, however, Serra's score was not only a failure in the film but a disgrace to the Bond tradition as a whole"[76] observed Christian Clemmensen on his 1996 review of the soundtrack album in

FilmTracks. The *GoldenEye* soundtrack, unlike many other elements of the film, presents a break between the old and the new Bond fans for its untraditional sound and singularity among the previous albums of the series, particularly those by John Barry. Much more traditional is the symphonic version of the "James Bond Theme" heard during the tank chase sequence and orchestrated by John Altman, called in after the original music Serra composed (available on the commercial soundtrack album, track 10) felt too cheesy and didn't provide the required dramatism for that scene.

In spite of the disagreement of some Bond music fans, nowadays it's hard to imagine a traditional sound for *GoldenEye* outside Serra's and the efforts of the Parisian composer turned out to be effective to create a post-Cold War atmosphere, and a welcome for James Bond into a new era. Composer Yannick Zenhäusern opines his music was perfect for the film: "It fit the movie like a glove. The whole dark and eerie undertone are perfectly accompanied by the equally industrial and experimental dark sounds of Eric Serra. It's clearly a product of the 1990s sonically, but in a good way." At the same time, Zenhäusern contradicts many fans and critics who think John Barry or David Arnold could have made a better work: "I don't want to imagine what *GoldenEye* would've sounded like with a score by David Arnold or John Barry. Fantastic, immensely talented composers. But the *GoldenEye* sound is Serra's baby."

GoldenEye would also set a generational milestone in the field of James Bond collecting since it was the first Bond film to get a DVD release. First commercialized in 1995, the Digital Versatile Disc was an improvement over the previous home video formats by allowing the user the access to behind-the-scenes material as well as picking a different language and subtitle tracks from a menu at their disposal. Similar characteristics to the LaserDisc format, but with an enhanced definition and sometimes the ability to change between the regular Pan&Scan format fit for standard TV screens or the original letterboxed presentation as seen on the big screen.[77] 007 debuted on this brand new format in North America on 26 March 1997 with *GoldenEye*, followed by classic titles like *Dr No*, *From Russia With Love* and *Goldfinger*. Although this edition only offered the film's theatrical trailer as an extra feature, two years later a Special Edition DVD would come with documentaries and featurettes, and in 2006 the film would get the two-disc set treatment with the Ultimate Edition collection, despite the movie itself received a much questionable digital "restoration" by Lowry where the frame was severely cropped and the colours were dramatically desaturated. Luckily, these mistakes were fixed for the BluRay edition in 2012.[78]

Much like many of the previous and future James Bond movies, *GoldenEye* is more than just an entertaining thriller and serves as a testimony of its times: a reflection of the politics, fashion, communications, technology and music of the mid-1990s camouflaged (or not so) beneath all the high-scale action sequences present in the film. Most action films may be regarded as a banal entertainment by some filmgoers, but the truth is that many of them represent a spirit, a way of doing gratifying action movies in a very special way that not even the most recent James Bond, *Mission: Impossible* or *Die Hard* outings were able to achieve.

GOLDENEYE AND FILMMAKING

"The novels by Ian Fleming were written in a visual style and Cubby (Broccoli) always said you could almost film the books,"[79] observed producer Michael G. Wilson in the book *The Art of Bond* by Laurent Bouzereau. And while *GoldenEye* is not based on an Ian Fleming novel or story, the film has an incredible visual style.

Not only the story of *GoldenEye* is fascinating and relevant for its times, but the film has a visual impact rarely seen in the James Bond series, although they all are known for being visually spectacular. The results seen on the big screen are the product of a very organized team effort in which all the areas worked with precision to deliver a solid James Bond film: the director, the screenwriters, the producers, the cast and the rest of the crew. A team effort which hasn't been seen since the 1960s with films like *Thunderball*, *You Only Live Twice* and *On Her Majesty's Secret Service*.

New Zealand-born director Martin Campbell took the helm of *GoldenEye* after the success of the 1985 BBC mini-series *Edge of Darkness*, a political thriller in which a London detective investigates the murder of his activist daughter through six one-hour chapters. Years later, Campbell had moderate success in Hollywood with films like *Criminal*

Law and *Defenseless* and actors like Gary Oldman and Barbara Hershey between 1988 and 1991. Then came the 1994 futuristic action movie *No Escape* (also known as *Escape From Absolom*), which wasn't well regarded by the critics. However, this film starring Ray Liotta and Lance Henriksen had an attractive visual style overall and daring action scenes. This has naturally turned the odds into Campbell's favour to direct the seventeenth James Bond adventure. Not in vain, *No Escape* was somehow the artistic blueprint for *GoldenEye*: detailed close-up shots of the actors faces and reactions abound in the 1994 movie, notably as Ray Liotta's Captain Robbins is thrown into a jungle surrounded by rats, or as the same character reflects on his past life sitting on a beach and looking at the horizon, something replicated in *GoldenEye* with Bond. The demise of Alec Trevelyan is also reminiscent of the death of the leading villain, Marek, played by Stuart Wilson, not forgetting the final shots of both movies where helicopters flying into the horizon in a jungle are featured.

Campbell's approach to simplify the communication among the cast and crew and to make sure everyone understood what he wanted for each major action scene consisted of the use of storyboards, commissioned to artist Martin Asbury. Naturally, the James Bond films were not new to the use of storyboards, but Campbell has given them special importance and he has regularly expressed a graphic version of the script has been useful for many of his projects: "The only way to get everything you want is to storyboard the action. You sit down with your stunt arranger/coordinator, discuss it, and figure out what you want," [80] he told author Andrew Lane in 2013.

The second unit of *GoldenEye* was in charge of Ian Sharp, whom Campbell recruited, in the know of his unique talent for action/adventure movies: "He came up to me at a screening. He said: 'I've been asked to do Bond, *GoldenEye*, and I don't want a stunt guy to do the second unit, would you do it?' He promised to do the second unit for me, which he never has done"[81], remembered Sharp in 2015 for *MI6 Confidential*. They knew each other from the days where both worked on the British TV series *The Professionals*, and Sharp proved he could be in charge of a whole action feature in 1982 when he directed *Who Dares Wins*, starring Lewis Collins from the aforementioned series. The second unit director was crucial in the supervision and coordination of scenes involving high-scale stunts like the opening bungee jump and the ground-breaking tank chase, while Campbell worked in other sequences involving the principal actors. Likewise, Simon Crane also deserves the credit for the stunt coordination of *GoldenEye*, a task he has carried away with great success after being part of the stunt team of *A View To A Kill*, *The Living Daylights* and *Licence To Kill*. The action scenes of *GoldenEye*, even the small ones, are very complex and yet perfectly choreographed, notably the shootout in the Military Archives and the initial scene at the nerve gas plant, two moments in the franchise that really have a characteristic Bond touch. A more escapist approach would be given by the stunt where 007 catches a falling Pilatus Porter plane in mid-air, a scene that was achieved by the stunt work of motorcyclist Jacques "Zoo" Malnuit and the legendary parachutist B.J. Worth, with the final touches completed by the model unit supervised by Derek Meddings.

The third unit of the film, or the model unit, has achieved a lot of the great work seen in the film, and Meddings' labour was so detailed that the human eye could barely notice the difference between a real object and a model on film, namely during the scene where a MiG fighter jet –affected by the GoldenEye blast– crashes into the Severnaya installation causing most of the destruction of the place. It was all done with scale-models, just like the images of the Petya and Mischa satellites over the Earth's orbit, or the antenna structure coming out of its hideout beneath the river, but it all looks very realistic and accurate when watching the film. Meddings, whose first Bond collaboration came in 1973 with *Live And Let Die*, sadly passed away shortly before the release of the film, which was dedicated to his memory.

Although *GoldenEye* would be the first Bond film to recur to CGI (Computer Generated Image) to touch up some details, the crew of the film wasn't too fond of overusing these new technologies, starting with Meddings: "Nowadays, unfortunately, people have got this thing in their heads that if they don't have access to a computer, the can't make films anymore," [82] he said. At the same time, visual effects supervisor Mara Bryan was pleased for the fact that both technologies were implemented in the movie: "There is a danger that the traditional techniques (…) will be ignored. This was certainly not the case on *GoldenEye*, where special and visual effects employed almost every known technique, old and new. It was very exciting to be part of it all"[83].

Martin Campbell, Ian Sharp, Simon Crane and Derek Meddings were basically the four big geniuses behind the production of *GoldenEye*, those who "made it happen" and could make the audience believe that what they see could be real, even if it was next to impossible or definitively impossible.

As for the aesthetic part of the film, *GoldenEye* has other geniuses, some of them regular collaborators of the Bond franchise and others brought by Campbell, known for rehiring many of the professionals who have worked with him in the past. The first one of Campbell's long-time collaborators was the director of photography, Phil Méheux, who has been his cinematographer of choice since 1988's *Criminal Law*. Editor Terry Rawlings, whose credits include *Chariots of Fire* and *Blade Runner*, has previously worked with Campbell in *No Escape*. It is believed that after the take on that film's action, he was probably a choice from the go by both the director and the producers. Production designer Peter Lamont and casting director Debbie McWilliams returned once more to the positions they had in the Bond saga since 1981's *For Your Eyes Only*. New additions to the team were second unit director Ian Sharp, costume designer Lindy Hemming, main title designer Daniel Kleinman (he directed Gladys Knight's "Licence To Kill" music video), soundtrack composer Eric Serra and the screenwriters: Jeffrey Caine and Bruce

Feirstein, who readapted Michael France's original screenplay (the latter got a "Story by" credit).

It is difficult to name a single responsible for the success of *GoldenEye* and is probably difficult to even name three people out of a crew where all deserve recognition. However, apart from director Martin Campbell who supervised everything, a special mention should go to Terry Rawlings and Phil Méheux, because of the tandem made by the cinematography and editing has been hard to beat by future Bond films.

The highlights of *GoldenEye*'s cinematography are the close-up and detail shots of the actors, notably during the first scene of Pierce Brosnan in the story, which brings back memories of *Dr No*. In the film that initiated the 007 series in 1962, we first see Sean Connery's hands dealing cards on a casino table before his face was revealed, saying the immortal "Bond, James Bond" introduction for the first time. Similarly, in *GoldenEye*, the well-known gun barrel sequence iris leads up to a striking shot of an enormous dam as an aeroplane passes by. Distant shots show us a man we are meant to believe is Bond running over the dam and taking a 640-feet bungee-jump (Brosnan was doubled by Wayne Michaels), then we see this shadowy man cutting through the rock to gain access to a secret installation, aided by a laser gun. As the man does the job, we are given a detail shot of his blue eyes. Later, as an unpreoccupied Soviet soldier gets into the toilet, we get more shots of this mysterious intruder who descents of the vent shaft to interrupt the soldier, comfortably reading the sports section of Pravda. As his face is revealed upside down, Bond smiles and says: "I beg your pardon. Forgot to knock," socking the living daylights out of him.

The close-ups are constant throughout the rest of the film. A good example can be seen during the reencounter between 007 and 006 in the Statue Park, as the camera zooms-in to former's eyes when he discovers the latter was not only alive and well, but was the mastermind behind it all. Other clever close shots are presented during the casino scene in Monaco, as Bond and Xenia face each other in a baccarat table, with the woman suggestively holding and smoking a cigar through her red lips. The cards being played are also prominently focused by the camera, enhancing the finesse of the moment. Near the end of the film, there is a clever and artistic take which, according to Martin Campbell, was inspired in *Waterworld* and *Apocalypse Now*: the reflection of Xenia Onatopp, rappelling down a helicopter over the jungle sunlight, is projected over the forehead of an unconscious Bond. This provides a sensation of mystery and suspense, which abruptly reaches an end when the woman violently lands by kicking 007 in the face.

Some of the most creative shots of Méheux's cinematography take place during quick sequences, as the supine take of Brosnan being frisked by a number of Janus' guards or the reflection of two missiles in his eyes (shades of the *Goldfinger* pre-credit sequence) as they come back right to blow the Tiger helicopter where he and Natalya are tied up. This category of unique visual achievement also includes the close-up on Bond's eyes as he tries to level off a plane falling through a cliff, or the tracking shot directed towards Trevelyan's mouth as the whole antenna structure falls over him. The director of photography used a similar resort in another two films directed by Martin Campbell, *The Mask of Zorro* and *The Legend of Zorro*, with the demise of the leading villains that confronted Antonio Banderas' version of the popular swashbuckler.

Another trademark of Phil Méheux was the use of chiaroscuro for three important sequences: Bond's infiltration on the nerve gas plant, the interrogation held at the Military Archives in St Petersburg, and the rendezvous between Bond and Alec Trevelyan on an abandoned and desolated statue park, for which Méheux took inspiration from the encounter between Holly Martins (Joseph Cotten) and Harry Lime (Orson Welles) in 1949's *The Third Man*, where the latter is hidden by the shadows and his face is briefly revealed by a small flash of light[84]. An interesting contrast is made between the desaturated cinematography for these scenes, comprised of washed-out colours (mostly grey, blue and green) and the one for the exotic locations, evidenced by a shiny palette: intense shades of blue and white to emphasise the richness of the Monaco harbour, vivid orange and yellow for the beach moments set in Cuba (shot in Puerto Rico) providing a sensation of heat, and the interior of the Casino de Monte Carlo, recreated by Peter Lamont at Leavesden studios, which enhances the luxury required for the scene with the use of brown, yellow and golden tones. Likewise, Janus' subterranean control centre takes full advantage of the "static" colours like green, blue and red.

The other part of this visual impact perceived *GoldenEye* is given by the dynamism of editor Terry Rawlings. Nominated for an Oscar in 1982 for his work on *Chariots of Fire*, Rawlings bears the distinction of being the first Bond editor to receive a credit on the film's theatrical posters. His job on the film's action scenes offers a necessary sharpness and precision to the story harkening back to the glory days of James Bond in the 1960s. Examples of this are Bond and Natalya running through the Military Archives as they avoid a rain of bullets from Ourumov's troops, as well as one of these enemy soldiers falling through a glass window into an office after being gunned down by a frenetic Bond. The hand-to-hand combat sequences are also enhanced by Rawlings' effective work, like the sauna fight, where Bond shows his quick reflexes by surprising Xenia Onatopp as she tries to attack him by the back. More close quarters combat scenes can be cited as an example of the editor's masterstroke: the fiery combat between 007 and 006 inside the Cuban antenna has the same dynamic pace as the scenes from the old Bond films like *On Her Majesty's Secret Service* and *From Russia With Love*.

A particular moment where both Méheux and Rawlings brilliantly combine their efforts takes place in a romantic scene: as Bond and Natalya kiss on a Cuban beach, their kiss fades into the hearth of the cottage in which they are then making love. This transition is a singular and very artistic move in which the fire symbolizes the concealed passion, which is now unleashed as this man and this woman, genuinely attracted to each other, share a fervent kiss.

Other creative points for the uniqueness of *GoldenEye* go to an old member of the Bond school, Peter Lamont. When the 007 Stage at Pinewood Studios was booked for the shooting of *First Knight*, starring Richard Gere and Sean Connery, the crew had to find a solution out of thin air. Lamont was given the task to come up with a new place to house the production and build the interiors. He took advantage of an area belonging to the former Rolls Royce factory at Leavesden Aerodrome, building a studio from scratch and –at the same time– building the sets for the film. Among those who look very elaborate and creative are the Soviet nerve gas plant, the Severnaya installation and the Janus base, where the production designer took plain advantage of cutting-edge technology relevant for the story, such as with huge TV screens, small monitors and computers all over the place. Another of Lamont's great achievements was a realistic recreation of the streets of St. Petersburg on the Leavesden backlot to shot most of the tank chase sequence, since the heavy vehicle could have seriously compromised the ancient structure of the former Leningrad city: "Walking on the set I'm amazed by the wonderfully detailed statues, made from glass fibre, which litter the glass (…) the detail on a set of this kind is quite amazing. Should you be transported from your bed and wake on this street, you could be forgiven for believing you were in Russia"[85] testified Graham Rye, editor of the popular *007 Magazine*, when invited to the set on June 1995.

A special mention must go to the screenplay of the film: the collaboration of four men that lead into a very imaginative and contemporary story. The one to come up with the great idea behind *GoldenEye* was screenwriter Michael France. Known for his work on the 1993 film *Cliffhanger*, starring Sylvester Stallone, France has been a James Bond fan for years and, during his teens, he edited a 007 fanzine. "We needed to treat Bond seriously and not to do one of the more comedic, sillier Bonds like *Moonraker*. By the same token, they didn't want to be as serious as *Licence To Kill*,"[86] he commented on his work on the script. France brought the key ideas of the movie, notably the rivalry between 007 and 006: "We'd never really gotten a serious look at another 00 agent. (…) I thought it would be interesting to get a look at a friendship and a betrayal, and just think about what would happen if one of these guys went bad. Somebody who had the same training as Bond and was just as clever as Bond, who decided to put that knowledge to work for himself"[87]

Another of Michael France's creations was the female antagonist, Xenia Onatopp, and the setting of Russia as a key location of the plot, which included an infiltration by Bond on the KGB Headquarters, ultimately discarded. British screenwriter Jeffrey Caine was hired later to work on France's original script, and he did some significant changes, like giving more relevance to Natalya Simonova (formerly Marina Varoskaya) and the outline of characters like Ourumov, Boris and Zukovsky, who were absent from the original screenplay.

France also did important research of hi-tech weaponry to find a suitable and contemporary plot to the film, until he found the prospect of an EMP satellite that could devastate technology. Producer Michael G. Wilson explains the nature of this innovative weapon: "The satellite is based on a Star Wars [SDI] weapon that was banned by a treaty between the US and Russia. It's a weapon left over the Cold War and is a first-strike system that can send a bomb from outer space that blows out all electronics within a large number of square miles. It's meant to knock out all of your command control systems so you can't respond to a nuclear attack. It also knocks out computers and technology of all kinds and can send a country back to the Stone Age."[88] In 1985's film *A View To A Kill*, James Bond played by Roger Moore briefly mentions the effect of an EMP blast to Frederick Gray, the film's fictional British Defence Minister.

After Jeffrey Caine handed in his last draft for *GoldenEye*, Kevin Wade was brought up to the project and he did some unaccredited work by touching up some dialogues, until American journalist and writer Bruce Feirstein did more important changes on the screenplay, turning it into the finished result seen on film. Upon request by director Martin Campbell, Feirstein turned M into a woman and rewrote some of the characters: he inspired Valentin on Signor Ferrari, played by Sidney Greenstreet in *Casablanca*, and made Boris younger and a geek. Also, his draft was overall outlined to show that the world has changed but Bond didn't. Much of the film's clever dialogues were also added by him, particularly some of Bond's interactions with Natalya ("Boys with toys"). Feirstein would continue his association with the series for the two following Brosnan Bond films, *Tomorrow Never Dies* and *The World Is Not Enough*, and he would also contribute for Bond video games like *Everything or Nothing*, *From Russia With Love* (based on the 1963 film) and *Blood Stone*, plus the remake of the original *GoldenEye 007* game in 2010.

Although recent James Bond films recruited Oscar winners in the cast, like Javier Bardem, Christoph Waltz and Rami Malek, the antagonists for Daniel Craig's 007 in *Skyfall*, *SPECTRE* and the upcoming and yet untitled Bond 25, that wasn't the case with the casting process for *GoldenEye*. The 1995 film was comprised by international artists like Sean Bean (England), Famke Janssen (The Netherlands), Izabella Scorupco (Poland), Robbie Coltrane (Scotland), Gottfried John (Germany) and Tcheky Karyo (France), who were relatively unknown outside their countries of origin or the places where they have previously acted. Many of them would, in fact, gain international recognition years later for their work in productions like *X-Men* or the HBO series *Games of Thrones*.

In *GoldenEye*, all these actors share memorable scenes with the new James Bond played by Pierce Brosnan, who was originally intended to follow Roger Moore after the London-born actor left the role with 1985's *A View To A Kill*.

Curiously, Moore and Brosnan shared more than the fame for a popular TV series before being James Bond: Brosnan's wife Cassandra Harris played a supporting Bond girl in Moore's film *For Your Eyes Only*. In fact, she was the one that "handed him in" to the role of James Bond during the premiere of the film in 1981. There, producer Cubby Broccoli thought he had the looks and charm to become the next 007 actor. In the end, contractual obligations with *Remington Steele* impeded Brosnan to take over the role in the very last minute, days before his original announcement as 007 in 1986. He went on with other roles that helped him shape the roughness needed for his Bond image, like the ruthless KGB agent Valeri Petrofsky in *The Fourth Protocol* or the FBI explosives expert Danny O'Neill in *Live Wire.* Sadly, between these years, Cassandra Harris died a victim of ovarian cancer in 1991.

Brosnan almost getting and then losing the role in 1986 got a lot of media attention, so the Irish actor was a bit worried of history repeating itself by April 1994, when Timothy Dalton announced his retirement. Some polls and journalists were already tipping him (yet again) for the role of Ian Fleming's secret agent: "When Tim left, it was like 'Here we go again.' When the subject came up, I just said to my agent, 'Look, I want this resolved as quickly as possible. I don't want to be part of a media circus. I want them –the studio, the company– to either say yes or no and that's it. (…) I don't need Bond in my life, but if they want to offer it to me, I'll definitely do it because it's like unfinished business.'"[89] Finally, on June 1, 1994, agent Fred Spector phoned his client and he said it all: "Hello, Mr Bond. You got the part!"[90] The actor remained tight-lipped for a week until he was formally introduced to the press on June 8, 1994, in a press conference held at the Regent Hotel in London.

Much like Terence Young did with Sean Connery for *Dr No*, Martin Campbell helped Pierce Brosnan to shape his James Bond persona to blend in with the times. "Pierce has been with the part for a long time now, and it's one that fits him like a glove. He's very underrated as an actor, too. Most people have his TV image of him, which comes with the often mistaken impression he's always doing second rate material. *GoldenEye* will correct that balance,"[91] Campbell explained to columnist Alan Jones from *Cinefantastique*, also detailing his outline for the action scenes involving the new Bond: "I keep massaging the whole project along by pushing him to always look cool under pressure and always handle the action in a calm and controlled way. (...) When he kills, he kills very hard and fast. I made all his actions very economic. One punch does it. It's just very simple and economic, no fussiness. I made him stand still a lot." [92]

Fans seemed to approve Pierce Brosnan even before he could be seen on the big screen as the world's most famous secret agent. Mark Cerulli, the producer of two official 007 documentaries, recalls the day he went to interview Brosnan with his team: "As he strode out to meet us, I remembered thinking it was as if James Bond had stepped right off the page", he told *MI6 Confidential*. He also said Brosnan was "warm, charming and seemed totally at ease, even tough for him, the professional stakes couldn't have been higher."[93] More good memories of Brosnan come from Derek Lyons, whose credits include the James Bond films *Octopussy*, *A View To A Kill* and *The Living Daylights*. A trained actor with a BA in Cinema and English, he was chosen at that point of his career to play a casino guest in *GoldenEye*, where he was reunited with Brosnan after appearing opposite him in productions like Guy Hamilton's *The*

Mirror Crack'd and *The Fourth Protocol*, plus an episode of TV's *Remington Steele*. Originally chosen to sit at the baccarat table, Lyons is ultimately seen among the casino guests: "When Pierce delivers his line, 'Bond... James Bond', I walk past him," he clarifies.

Lyons remembers that there was regularly a lot of pressure on the set since the filmmakers knew that the success of the film would define the future of the series. However, he points out that Brosnan always cool and a sympathetic man: "I told him that I was very sad to hear his wife had died. He told me: 'That's very kind of you, Derek, I appreciate it'". The actor also thanked him for congratulating him for becoming James Bond after the chance he missed back in 1986. The only moment where he remembers the Irish star being a bit unhappy was on the last day of shooting when his personal gold watch was stolen: "I think it was his own one, gold Rolex I think it was. Someone stole it. A few weeks later they found out it was one of the crew".

The rest of the artists involved in *GoldenEye* stand out for turning out to be extremely talented despite most of them didn't have a Hollywood or Oscar-influenced background. Both leading ladies are fantastic in opposing roles: Izabella Scorupco as the good girl, the victim, the innocent entangled on an international conspiracy; and Famke Janssen as the deathly *femme fatale* – provocative, cruel, and ruthless.

The same can be said about the villains: Sean Bean, who has previously antagonized Harrison Ford's Jack Ryan in *Patriot Games*, is cynical and spiteful in the role of Alec Trevelyan, "the man who knows him (Bond) better", according to the film promotions; and there's also Gottfried John, stone-faced and threatening enough to represent the old Soviet glory embodied in General Ourumov. Every actor has certainly owned their respective role and is at this point almost impossible to think of a suitable replacement for any of them. The same can be said of the supporting cast, where three actors stand out particularly for the amount of humour they provide to the film: Alan Cumming as hacker Boris Grishenko, Robbie Coltrane as ex-KGB agent Valentin Zukovsky and Joe Don Baker as CIA agent Jack Wade, sent to collaborate with Bond in St Petersburg. The latter two turned out to be very appreciated by the fans and reprised their roles in subsequent Brosnan Bond films: Coltrane made a final appearance in *The World Is Not Enough*, while Baker did it in *Tomorrow Never Dies*, resulting in his third Bond film after playing arms dealer Brad Whitaker, who confronted Timothy Dalton in 1987's *The Living Daylights*.

The major change inside the usual MI6 team came, of course, with the casting of Judi Dench as M and Samantha Bond as Moneypenny. The only one who did not leave, however, was the legendary Desmond Llewelyn on his 15th appearance as the gadget master Q. While James Bond is played by a different actor, having Llewelyn back in the role provides a tranquil sense of continuity in *GoldenEye*, as if one could see that this Bond and this Q have known each other for years. Llewelyn commented about his role in *GoldenEye* that "Q would probably not like to see a foreign car, the

BMW, used by Bond and he would not approve of a female M, either. That's how he is: old fashioned in a changing world"[94].

This would be one of the three last contributions of Llewelyn in the series, before his much-lamented death in December 1999, a month after the release of *The World Is Not Enough*. The character was replaced by John Cleese in *Die Another Day* and discontinued until Ben Whishaw played him opposite Daniel Craig's 007 in *Skyfall* and *SPECTRE*.

GoldenEye also reintroduced the character of Bill Tanner, considered as Bond's best friend in the Service in the Ian Fleming novels, played here by British character actor Michael Kitchen. The MI6's Chief of Staff made several appearances in the novels, but he was reduced to a rather bossy portrayal as M's replacement in *For Your Eyes Only*, played by James Villiers, and to a small speaking part in *The Man With The Golden Gun*, played by Michael Goodliffe. Kitchen's portrayal is probably the most convincing of them all, as evidenced by the scene in which he and Bond share a joke on the new M, indicating there is a real friendship between the two outside of the service. After one more appearance by Kitchen in *The World Is Not Enough*, Rory Kinnear took over the same role in the Craig era, starting with *Quantum of Solace*, although his character lacks the same dynamics with Bond that Kitchen had.

This film was also the formal debut of Michael G. Wilson and Barbara Broccoli as the producers in charge of the franchise. The duo proved that they had what it takes to carry on with the Bond torch after the death of the legendary Albert R. "Cubby" Broccoli in 1996, keeping the cinematic legacy of 007 alive.

GoldenEye is a unique visual feast, an invitation for adventure, and an example of solid teamwork, all under the leadership of Martin Campbell, who not only was hired to introduce a new James Bond in 2006's *Casino Royale*, but he seems to be the fans' favourite every time the hunt for a new Bond director is on. Although they were little known throughout the world, every one of the actors excelled in their roles, showing that sometimes there is a lot of unexplored talent outside Hollywood and the Academy. Some of the most remarkable sequences of the movie lay on people like Phil Méheux and Terry Rawlings, whose dynamism behind the cameras helped to make *GoldenEye* extremely watchable and enjoyable.

Apart from saving the James Bond franchise, *GoldenEye* brought back the visual richness that made James Bond a spectacle best viewed on a giant screen.

GOLDENEYE
AND THE VIDEO GAMES

James Bond has never been a stranger to video games, and adaptations of the 007 films (or original stories featuring Bond) to gaming platforms date back to 1983 with the first game starring Ian Fleming's secret agent for platforms like ColecoVision and Atari 2600, developed by Parker Brothers. Between the late 1980s and early 1990s, Domark produced games based on *Live And Let Die*, *The Spy Who Loved Me*, *The Living Daylights* and *Licence To Kill*, not forgetting the original storyline of *James Bond 007: The Duel* for the Sega console systems in 1993. However, every expert on the subject will agree that Bond didn't become a phenomenon in the field of interactive games until the Nintendo 64 adaptation of *GoldenEye*, developed by Rareware and released on August 25, 1997, to financial and critical success.

Development of the game began in January 1995, just as the film was starting production. It was initially planned for the Super Nintendo and Virtual Boy consoles as a 2D, which then evolved into a Nintendo 64 version with a 3D environment[95]. Martin Hollis, director of the project, and his team of developers, who had little to no experience in the making of video games, were allowed to visit the film sets designed by Peter Lamont and get copies of the blueprints in order to replicate each game scenario to the detail. Apart from *GoldenEye*, the game also homages earlier James Bond films with the inclusion of classic Bond villains like Jaws, Baron Samedi, Oddjob and May Day in the multiplayer mode, two of them also taking part in bonus missions of the single-player campaign. Early game footage shows that previous Bond actors (Connery, Moore and Dalton) were available in the multiplayer mode, but they were scrapped out to avoid copyright issues and paying royalties to each of the actors.

Inspiration for *GoldenEye 007* came from Sega's *Virtua Cop*, originally planned as an on-rails shooter where civilian casualties from the player were punished. Later, the game veered more into the *Doom* territory with the first-person perspective. The launch title for the Nintendo 64 console, *Super Mario 64*, served as the multi-objective base of the game: the player has to achieve the completion of several tasks in order to move forward through the 18 levels based on the film's screenplay. Despite all the effort invested, the game didn't perform well at the E3 exposition in 1997, and the fact that it was attached to a film released two years earlier didn't help: "No-one who played it at the show seemed terribly impressed. Worse, most people just walked by without playing,"[96] reflected Hollis on a document presented for the 2004 European Developers Forum. Many reviewers were also discouraged for the prospect of a first-person shooter for a console instead of PC, as it was the norm with games like *Doom*, *Wolfstein 3D* or *Quake*.

In the end, and against every prediction, the game was a huge success, selling around 2.1 million units in a year and grossing over $250 million worldwide. On his 1997 review, Doug Perry from the popular video gaming site *IGN* said: "*GoldenEye 007* is an intelligently conceived and brilliantly executed diamond of a game, building its spy-style adventure smartly on the foundation of the first-person genre, and unleashing the full power of Nintendo's four-player capabilities (...) In fact, we can say with a clear conscience that *GoldenEye 007* is the best single-player first-person game on any system."[97] *GameSpot*, another popular video game portal, also praised the game, giving it a 9.8 rating: "*GoldenEye* is the type of game N64 owners have been waiting for since they finished *Mario 64*. It has outstanding graphics and sound, and contains a certain depth in its gameplay that really entices you to finish it on all three difficulty levels."[98]

More than 20 years after its release, *GoldenEye 007* is tipped by many as the father of the modern first-person shooters and in 2007 *GamePro* ranked it ninth among the 52 most important video games of all time[99]. This product has a number of conditions missing in today's interactive adventures, including those of James Bond: it's challenging, funny, entertaining and very replayable – the completion of time trials in order to unlock cheats kept young players hooked into their Nintendo 64 consoles for entire afternoons, at the same time the multiplayer mode (added in the nick of time) increased the popularity of the game sky high.

Hollis attributed part of the success of this product to the unplanned nature of the level design, which gave the game a much appreciated non-linear feel: "There are rooms with no direct relevance to the level. There are multiple routes across the level. This is an anti-game design approach, frankly. It is inefficient because much of the level is unnecessary to the gameplay. But it contributes to a greater sense of freedom, and also realism. And in turn, this sense of freedom and realism contributed enormously to the success of the game."[100]

GoldenEye 007 followed the storyline of the film very closely, but the script by David Doak (who makes a memorable cameo as a scientist on the second mission) added some levels to expand the original experience and give Bond more participation for the sake of playability. "In the game, James Bond goes everywhere, unlike the film," Hollis told the *N64 Anthology* project in 2016. "I'd say three-quarters of the film is in the game (...). By sticking too close to the film, there's a risk of becoming too didactic, even too pedantic in the sequencing."[101]

The game begins just like the film, with the very first level based on the Arkangel mission in 1986. The player, controlling Bond, has to get into a secret chemical weapons facility by bungee-jumping over the Byelomorye Dam in the USSR. While in the film this scene is brief, Bond here has to confront a number of guards and (depending on the difficulty) install a covert modem on a mainframe. Mission two takes place on the aforementioned facility and results in the death of Alec Trevelyan by Ourumov, as Bond escapes on an aeroplane through the complex's runway in the third level. Things change in the following missions: it is 1991 and Bond is sent to Severnaya, Russia, to investigate a satellite control station. After deactivating the communications link to the place, Bond infiltrates the installation's bunker, where he makes a copy of the GoldenEye key and forces hacker Boris Grishenko to disable the security from the mainframe terminal. Of course, James Bond has never been in Severnaya in the film, but the developers decided to take some creative licence to allow the player the exploration of more environments seen in the movie. Seemingly unrelated to the film is mission six, set in 1993 where Bond is sent to Kyrgyzstan to investigate an unscheduled test firing of a missile, a cover for the launch of the GoldenEye satellite. Ourumov ambushes Bond, but he manages to escape as the secret agent blows the missile silo away with C4 explosives. In the briefing pages, Q makes a reference to agent 004 being a victim of these explosives in Beirut, which sounds like an event taking place in 1974's *The Man With The Golden Gun*, where 002 is said to be shot by the villain Francisco Scaramanga in Beirut. This was, most likely, a poetic licence.

The seventh level is the first one set in 1995 and is once again inspired by the events of the film. James Bond has to intervene in a hostage situation at the frigate La Fayette in Monte Carlo, where the Janus crime syndicate has taken hostages and placed explosives. After rescuing the hostages and defusing the bombs, 007 plants a tracker bug on the Pirate helicopter (named Tiger in the film) and escapes. The mission briefing indicates Xenia Onatopp is on board, just like in the movie, but there is no trace of her in the whole map. The game continues with Bond returning to Severnaya again, where he is captured and placed into the bunker's cells. This is where he meets Natalya, also captive and accused of treason. Aided by his magnetic gadget watch, Bond escapes with Natalya before the bunker is blown to bits by the GoldenEye weapon and then goes to a statue park in St. Petersburg, where he meets ex-KGB agent Valentin Zukovsky. This man arranges a blind date with Janus near the Lenin statue. Bond goes to the Lenin statue and, just like in the movie, he learns that Janus is none other than Alec Trevelyan, who has faked his death and switched sides. This time, he sets the Pirate helicopter to detonate with Natalya unconscious by its side. After rescuing her, Bond is arrested with Natalya by Defence Minister Dimitri Mishkin, who takes them to the GRU Military Archives.

Shooting his way out, Bond escapes interrogation with Natalya and they both meet Mishkin, now aware of Bond's claim of Ourumov's betrayal, handing him the Pirate helicopter black box. After they escape the archives, Natalya is captured by Ourumov. Bond gives chase through the streets of St. Petersburg: the player can opt to do it by sprinting or to grab the tank as in the movie. Some difficulties require Bond to meet Valentin Zukovsky again to contact his associates to "delay" Ourumov's car. Reaching an arms depot used by Janus, Bond destroys his weapons cache and gets into Trevelyan's ICBM train. Eliminating a number of heavily-armoured troops and bodyguards through each carriage, he finds Trevelyan, his henchwoman Xenia, and Ourumov who is holding Natalya at gunpoint. 007 kills Ourumov and, as Natalya locates Janus' base, finds a way out of the carriage before the bomb set by Trevelyan detonates in one minute.

Trained on firearms by Jack Wade (who is never seen in the game, but regularly mentioned), Natalya accompanies Bond to Cuba. Their plane is shot down and they perform a ground search of Janus' base, evading guards and confronting Xenia, who is shot by Bond. After destroying the gun emplacements, the duo gets into Janus' Control Centre, where Natalya uses her knowledge to disrupt the GoldenEye satellite, forcing it to burn into the Earth atmosphere. As Natalya escapes, Bond follows Trevelyan through subterranean caverns until they both reach the antenna cradle, where the former agent 006 will try to reactivate the GoldenEye satellite. Bond manages to destroy the GoldenEye control console, as he eliminates Trevelyan on a platform above the dish, sending his old friend to his demise with gunshots.

The game ends with Bond kissing Natalya on the Cuban jungle, although when beaten on higher difficulties two missions inspired in two Roger Moore Bond films will be unlocked: Aztec, where Bond has to reprogram a space shuttle belonging to the Drax Corporation while facing off Jaws (*Moonraker*), and Egyptian, where Bond has to recover Francisco Scaramanga's Golden Gun from an ancient temple and eliminate Baron Samedi (*Live And Let Die* and *The Man With The Golden Gun*).

GoldenEye 007 set the template for future James Bond video games: after the critical failure of Electronic Arts' *Tomorrow Never Dies* for PlayStation, which was a third-person game, the California-based video game studio that got the Bond licence in 1998 returned to the first-person perspective for the three following 007 games: *The World Is Not Enough*, based on the 1999 film and released for both PlayStation and Nintendo 64, and the original adventures *Agent Under Fire*, and *007 Nightfire*, made for the sixth generation of video game consoles like PlayStation 2 and GameCube. Nevertheless, none of them could beat the success of *GoldenEye 007* or its popularity.

In 2004, Electronic Arts developed a James Bond universe spin-off titled *GoldenEye: Rogue Agent*, in which the player controlled a renegade MI6 agent kicked out for reckless and unnecessary brutality. After losing an eye on a confrontation with Dr No, the renegade operative joins Auric Goldfinger and Francisco Scaramanga, who is on an internal battle with Dr No's organization. The protagonist gets a cybernetic golden eye implanted in the place of his right eye and is subsequently nicknamed "GoldenEye" by Pussy Galore, who teams up with him on his many missions against Dr No's sidekicks like Xenia Onatopp.

Writers Danny Bilson and Paul DeMeo reduced the appearance of James Bond (not bearing the likeness of any of the actors) to a short cameo at the beginning of the story during a virtual reality training mission inspired by the Fort Knox scene from *Goldfinger*. The rest of the game dealt with the original story lead by this rogue agent nicknamed GoldenEye, who (according to the game's tag line) wonders about the point of saving the world if he can rule it.

The approach of this game was original and innovative in terms of story, and it counted with the collaboration of legendary production designer Ken Adam, who made futuristic versions of his classic Bond sets for the game levels, but *GoldenEye: Rogue Agent* wasn't well received by the critics. *GameSpot*'s Jeff Gerstmann, who praised the Nintendo 64 original, gave this spin-off a lukewarm 6.3 rating, complained about the "uninteresting story and lacklustre gameplay."[102] Doug Perry from *IGN* was even tougher, calling it "an empty vessel of a game missing personality, charm, story or any kind of distinguishing character" and sentencing that "if video games were living creatures and had souls, *Rogue Agent* would be the wandering game in search of one."[103] Ultimately, this game passed to history was only a poor move to use the name of a very popular and successful James Bond game to deliver a rather shabby product. Meanwhile, something more interesting was being planned on the Microsoft front, with an XBOX Live Arcade version of the original *GoldenEye 007* game with improved graphics, planned for a 2007 release. Unfortunately, the project was cancelled in the nick of time when Rareware and Nintendo didn't reach an agreement on money, as composer Grant Kirkhope pointed out[104].

That was not, however, the end of the road for the resurgence of the title *GoldenEye* in the world of video gaming.

Owners of the licence of the James Bond video games since 2008 and making their debut with the adaptation of *Quantum of Solace*, Activision announced at the 2010 E3 exposition a remake of *GoldenEye 007* for Nintendo Wii, this time with the story updated to the current times and with the voice and likeness of Daniel Craig as James Bond. The characters of Alec Trevelyan, General Ourumov, Natalya Simonova, Xenia Onatopp and Valentin Zukovsky were provided with a different likeness to those of the original actors. Much in the style of modern James Bond games, this Wii version of *GoldenEye 007* is more cinematic than the original, featuring mind-blowing sets designed by Robert Cowper, a soundtrack by Kevin Kiner with cues by David Arnold, and a very Bondian main title sequence with Tina Turner's "GoldenEye" now performed by Nicole Scherzinger, from The Pussycat Dolls.

Written by Bruce Feirstein, one of the scribes of the 1995 film, the new *GoldenEye* begins in the present day with James Bond and Alec Trevelyan, agent 006, infiltrating a chemical weapons facility in Archangel, Russia, gaining access through a nearby dam. It is believed that the man in charge of the facility, a high ranking Russian General named Arkady Ourumov, is being the source of weapons for a terrorist organization targeting British embassies across the globe. After their presence is spotted, Trevelyan manages to parachute off the dam while Bond uses his parachute to distract the guards and jumps off unprotected, managing to break his fall by sliding over the dam's concrete and falling into the water.

Both agents reunite inside the facility and, as Bond plants explosives over the complex, Trevelyan is captured and killed by Ourumov. 007 escapes by using a bike on the installation's airfield and catching a plane falling uncontrolled in mid-air, just like in the original film. Later, MI6 intercepts a call between Ourumov and Russian gangster Valentin

Zukovsky, whom Bond previously confronted, giving him a scar in his right cheek. The General is trying to acquire a helicopter modified to survive an EMP blast. Bond goes to Zukovsky's nightclub in Barcelona and Zukovsky directs him to a floating arms fair in Dubai. Later, he's shot down by one of the waitresses, revealed to be Xenia Onatopp, a known associate of Ourumov. Framed as Zukovsky's killer, Bond evades the bodyguards and escapes before the police arrive.

007 arrives in Dubai and spots Ourumov and Xenia, who shoot down Sky Briggs, head of security of the event, and take hostages in order to divert Bond from stopping them as they steal the EMP-hardened helicopter. Before they escape, he manages to plant his cell phone tracker in the helicopter. The British Secret Service tracks the phone to a remote base in Siberia, where the GoldenEye weapon satellite is detonated before he can infiltrate the place. As Ourumov and Xenia escape, 007 rescues computer programmer Natalya Simonova, one of the intended victims of the blast. Later, they are both arrested by the Russian army, thought to have been involved in the incident. The duo is taken to the St. Petersburg Military Archives, where Defence Minister Dimitri Mishkin interrogates them. After Natalya accuses Ourumov of stealing the weapon and detonating it over the base, the General appears, shoots Mishkin and abducts Natalya.

Bond escapes from the Archives and pursues Ourumov's Humvee with a tank through the streets of St. Petersburg. Eventually, he reaches an armoured train, which he derails. Infiltrating the train, he finds Xenia and

Ourumov, as a guard is holding Natalya at gunpoint. Bond confronts them about the plans for the GoldenEye satellite, seeding the distrust between each other. The trick works: Xenia betrays Ourumov and shoots him. As Bond frees Natalya, Xenia throws them a grenade, setting the carriage on fire. They make a miraculous escape in time.

Natalya tells 007 that she has overheard Ourumov scheduling a meeting with someone at a memorial statue park near the region. Bond visits the park and, after some exploration, he finds Alec Trevelyan, who reveals to have survived the facility explosion and is now Janus, the man behind the GoldenEye theft. Unlike the original film and the game, Trevelyan's reason for betrayal is now the banking system and the government agencies that make a profit of soldiers and agents who are no longer able to fight for Queen and Country. After a long speech, Trevelyan knocks Bond off with a sleeping dart and ties him on the EMP resistant helicopter, rigged to explode. At the same time, he has captured Natalya who is crucial for the completion of his plan.

Bond escapes and follows Trevelyan's lead to a solar plant in Nigeria. Exploring the place through the air, his aeroplane is shot down and he continues on foot, evading Janus' forces and eliminating Xenia Onatopp (in a similar way to the film) on the process. Eventually, Bond gains access to the solar plant. Trevelyan is attempting to use the GoldenEye to eliminate every trace of banking records after making online transfers, but Bond tricks him into destroying his computers. Bond rescues Natalya, overloads the control room of the solar plant and fights Trevelyan atop a platform, where he quickly shoots him, sending his former friend over the tower. The game ends with Bond and Natalya kissing in the Nigerian jungle.

This new version of *GoldenEye 007* was also critically acclaimed: "Despite a few problems in the multiplayer department, *GoldenEye 007* is a great game that does justice to its prestigious name. Instead of living in the past, Bond's latest adventure embraces the present. The explosive single-player campaign is an incredible ride all the way through, and it's well worth replaying a few times just to see what sort of cool secrets the harder difficulties hide,"[105] commented Tom Mc Shea from *GameSpot*, who gave the game an 8.5 rating. *IGN*'s Craig Harris was even keener to the reworking of the story: "What could have ended up a game that cruised on autopilot and simply relied on a name to sell it has turned out to be one of the best first-person shooters on Wii,"[106] he said giving the game with a solid 9.0 overall rating. In 2011, the game would be given a high-definition version for PlayStation 3 and XBOX 360, titled *GoldenEye 007: Reloaded*.

Although this revival of *GoldenEye 007* proved the strong legacy left by the original in the video gaming world, which was crucial to the success of the post-1995 James Bond films and games, the Activision version will always fall short when compared to the original. While the story has been cleverly updated by none other than Bruce Feirstein, screenwriter of the original film, many gamers that grew up with the Nintendo 64 classic will agree that this 2010 version loses all the fun and magic of Rareware's original, much of the complaints aiming to the linear playability opposed to the somewhat "sandbox" nature of the 1997 version.

Ben Colclough, a freelance 3D artist who is currently working on the *GoldenEye 25* project (disclosed later in this chapter), is one of the biggest critics of Activision's *GoldenEye 007*: "The 2010 game didn't revolutionize anything. It simply borrowed the well-established *Call of Duty* formula and applied it to the Bond universe. It seems as if many modern first-person shooters games don't want the player to think or make observations by themselves. A mini-map reveals the number and location of enemies. On-screen waypoints tell the player exactly where to go and what to do at almost all times. All these factors combine to discourage exploration, which is one of my favourite parts of any first-person shooter game. All in all, I'd say it was a disappointingly mediocre game for many of us *GoldenEye* fans."

Although this remake wasn't well received by most of the old-school gamers, the love for the original version game has generated fascinating fan projects where talented 3D artists and developers have invested their time to make justice to the 1997 legend. A notorious example is *GoldenEye: Source*, a free recreation of the game's famous multiplayer mode using the *Half-Life* engine. Created by Nicholas "Nickster" Bishop in 2005, this mod was listed among the top ten of fan-remade classics by *PC Gamer* in 2014[107]. With its last major update in August 2016, *GoldenEye: Source* is up and running and is considered by many as the spiritual heir of the multiplayer part of the original game.

Another fan project who is eagerly awaited is *GoldenEye 25*, developed by Ben Colclough and with original music by Yannick Zenhäusern, both part of the *GoldenEye: Source* team. Set for an August 2022 release, to commemorate the 25th anniversary of the Nintendo 64 classic, *GoldenEye 25* is a non-commercial recreation of the original for PC, modelled after the *Unreal 4* engine. Made by two people that grew up with both the film and the game, this project is intended to homage both of them, giving the player a fully cinematic experience, which was missing in the original due to the Nintendo 64 limitations. Most level layouts, thankfully, will be almost identical to those of the original game. In conversation with *The Bond Bulletin*, Colclough promised to take full advantage of the new technologies to improve some tiny details that were missing from the original: "The changes are largely visual. In some cases, I'll add more environmental detail. For example, the dish and surrounding jungle will be added to Cradle."[108] At the same time, while Zenhäusern has said that he loves the music of the original game, composed by Grant Kirkhope and Graeme Norgate, he stressed that his score for *GoldenEye 25* will be heavily influenced by Eric Serra's work in the original film: "Now, the gaming experience with its redefined graphics is leaning closer towards the film, so why shouldn't the music do the same?" [109]

Thanks to its video game versions, *GoldenEye* is now not only associated with a 1995 James Bond film, but with a legend of the video games that marked a generation. The game introduced many people to the film, and the fact that the name *GoldenEye* is still high sounding in the gaming world is a great benefit for the entire Bond franchise, particularly to the films of the Pierce Brosnan era. As the movie is approaching its silver anniversary, it's fair to say that its video game versions have played a crucial role to immortalize the film and James Bond for the modern times.

THE LEGACY OF GOLDENEYE

It's hard to believe that almost 25 years have passed since Pierce Brosnan made its James Bond debut and that everyone who has spent hours playing the *GoldenEye* game for hours in their Nintendo 64 consoles is definitely not a kid anymore. Incredibly enough, the cinematic James Bond franchise will celebrate its 60th anniversary in only three years! This fact leaves the last chapter of this book to reflect on the legacy of *GoldenEye* and to take a look at how this film aged in more than two decades.

GoldenEye was a commercial success and most of the critics were generous to the movie, notably the famous Roger Ebert who defended the film on his TV show against his co-host Gene Siskel, who wasn't really convinced of the changes implemented to the James Bond character[110]. Michael Wilmington, from the *Chicago Tribune*, praised Pierce Brosnan's portrayal, pointing out that "the new Agent 007 (...) delivers whatever Bond devotees could reasonably want, or what newcomers anticipate" and that he "has everything the part needs: looks, charm, brains, a light touch, a suggestion of inner ruthlessness."[111] *CNN*'s Carol Buckland also reacted positively to the film: "James Bond's latest outing is big, and it's brash – in short, it's double-oh-fun. (...) All in all, *GoldenEye* is good, retro-style entertainment. It polishes up the 007 franchise in slick style. Bond will live on, at least for one more sequel."[112]

Instead of passing into history as just another James Bond film, *GoldenEye* leapt into immortality with the help of a much-acclaimed video game adaptation for Nintendo 64 in 1997. The success of this product progressed into a retroactive appraisal for the original film due to the similarities with the story and characters that became very popular. And while the 2010 remake version of this video game wasn't very much liked by fans, it ended up proving that the template of the story could still work when adapted to the 21st century or Daniel Craig's portrayal of the secret agent. *GoldenEye* was also the path to international stardom for artists like Famke Janssen, Alan Cumming and Sean Bean, which were already popular in their countries but relatively unknown worldwide. It did also establish Martin Campbell as a very prolific director for action movies and thrillers who would later go on to direct the cinematic return of Johnston McCulley's the famous swashbuckler Zorro two times given his success with James Bond.

On an interesting note, the influence of *GoldenEye* is heavily perceived on the 1998 film *The Mask of Zorro*, where many action sequences and even situations along the story seem lifted from the 1995 Bond film: notably a hero who is eager to avenge the death of his brother and is anxious to kill the man responsible, an American captain, which is quite reminiscent to 007's concealed desire to eliminate General Ourumov, who shot his then-friend Trevelyan, throughout the movie.

GoldenEye actors like Izabella Scorupco, Pierce Brosnan and Simon Kunz would also return to serve under Campbell's orders in movies like *Vertical Limit* and *The Foreigner*, released in 2000 and 2017. So the influence of this film has had a notable impact on the career of this director. And given his success with *GoldenEye*, he was the first man the Bond bosses had in mind when the arduous task of introducing a new 007 actor and rebooting the franchise with the 2006 adaptation of Ian Fleming's first Bond novel *Casino Royale*, a task he achieved passing with flying colours.

However, the most important thing 007 fans and filmgoers owe to *GoldenEye* is that it resurrected James Bond. It was a fresh rebirth for the character that Ian Fleming, Albert R. Broccoli and Harry Saltzman had conceived in different ways and the film had the right measures of ingredients to please old and new audiences. The six-year gap that had fans desperate was paid back in full with an outstanding, dynamic, rich and eye-popping adventure that stressed that our hero was back, while at the same time welcoming new generations of Bond fans that grew up as the Internet was slowly becoming part of our lives and this huge world became every day smaller.

Many critics predicted that Bond was past his sell-by date and that he had no place in the 1990s. Thanks to *GoldenEye*, they were proved wrong. And the film is the testimony that a hero like James Bond is, without doubt, a man for all seasons, a popular icon that could never be typecasted into a particular decade or political climate, and that still has a lot to offer as the world is in constant evolution. The teaser trailer itself made echo of this idea: "It's a new world, with new threats and new enemies. But you can still depend on one man…"

Last but not least, the film stands as a tribute to many members of the cast and crew that have departed in the past two decades: Albert R. Broccoli, Derek Meddings, Desmond Llewelyn, Michael France, Gottfried John and Terry Rawlings, all immortalized in every frame of the film or in every tiny detail of its unique brilliance. And, for many Bond fans *GoldenEye* is a unique film even inside the uniqueness of the series as a whole. It's the movie that has the effect of a time machine, drifting them to the golden days of their childhood, making every watch –no matter where or in which format– feel like the first time. For any 1990s kid, it's just impossible not to smile whenever it pops up on TV or to tune out until the end, even if they have seen it hundreds of times.

Half of everything was luck. The other half was fate. And sometimes, luck and fate can both combine to produce a timeless classic, an icon that represents a generation, proving at the same time that every time we see the words "James Bond Will Return" at the end of every Bond film, we are not reading just a cliché but a fervent promise by a team of talented and devoted filmmakers.

A quarter of a century after its release, *GoldenEye* keeps proving that there is *still* no substitute.

GOLDENEYE FACT SHEET

RELEASE DATE / 17 November 1995

RUNNING TIME / 130 minutes

DIRECTOR / Martin Campbell

PRODUCERS / Michael G. Wilson and Barbara Broccoli

SCREENPLAY / Michael France (Story), Jeffrey Caine and Bruce Feirstein.

PRODUCTION DESIGNER / Peter Lamont

DIRECTOR OF PHOTOGRAPHY / Phil Méheux BSC

EDITOR / Terry Rawlings

COSTUME DESIGNER / Lindy Hemming

MUSIC BY / Eric Serra

MAIN TITLE SONG PERFORMED BY / Tina Turner (written by Bono & The Edge)

THE CAST

PIERCE BROSNAN (James Bond) / SEAN BEAN (Alec Trevelyan) / IZABELLA SCORUPCO (Natalya Simonova) / FAMKE JANSSEN (Xenia Onatopp) / JOE DON BAKER (Jack Wade) / JUDI DENCH (M) / ROBBIE COLTRANE (Valentin Zukovsky) / TCHEKY KARYO (Dimitri Mishkin) / GOTTFRIED JOHN (General Ourumov) / ALAN CUMMING (Boris Grishenko) / DESMOND LLEWELYN (Q) / SAMANTHA BOND (Miss Moneypenny) / MICHAEL KITCHEN (Bill Tanner) / SERENA GORDON (Caroline) / SIMON KUNZ (Severnaya Duty Officer)

THE JAMES BOND FILMS

- *Dr No* (1962)
- *From Russia With Love* (1963)
- *Goldfinger* (1964)
- *Thunderball* (1965)
- *You Only Live Twice* (1967)
- *On Her Majesty's Secret Service* (1969)
- *Diamonds Are Forever* (1971)
- *Live And Let Die* (1973)
- *The Man With The Golden Gun* (1974)
- *The Spy Who Loved Me* (1977)
- *Moonraker* (1979)
- *For Your Eyes Only* (1981)
- *Octopussy* (1983)
- *A View To A Kill* (1985)
- *The Living Daylights* (1987)
- *Licence To Kill* (1989)
- *GoldenEye* (1995)
- *Tomorrow Never Dies* (1997)
- *The World Is Not Enough* (1999)
- *Die Another Day* (2002)
- *Casino Royale* (2006)
- *Quantum of Solace* (2008)
- *Skyfall* (2012)
- *SPECTRE* (2015)
- Bond 25* (2020)

Other James Bond films (not made by EON Productions):

- *Casino Royale* (1954 – TV film)
- *Casino Royale* (1967)
- *Never Say Never Again* (1983)

*Film in production, title not defined as of May 2019.

GOLDENEYE TIMELINE

April 1993: Michael France is hired to write the tentatively-titled Bond 17 adventure, which would be Timothy Dalton's third James Bond film.

August 1993: Michael France hands in a second draft for Bond 17.

January 1994: Michael France finishes his work on Bond 17, now titled *GoldenEye*.

April 11, 1994: Timothy Dalton announces his retirement of the role of James Bond.

June 1, 1994: Pierce Brosnan receives a phone call from his agent Fred Spector: "Hello, Mr Bond. You got the part!"

June 8, 1994: Pierce Brosnan is unveiled to the world press at the as the new James Bond, to star in *GoldenEye*, originally set for a summer 1995 release.

November 30, 1994: Dutch actress Famke Janssen joins the cast of *GoldenEye* in the role of Xenia Onatopp.

January 16, 1995: Production begins on *GoldenEye*, shooting the encounter between James Bond and Valentin Zukovsky.

January 22, 1995: The principal cast of *GoldenEye* is introduced to the world press in an event held at Leavesden Studios.

January 29, 1995: Shooting begins in Puerto Rico, doubling for Cuba in *GoldenEye*.

February 7, 1995: Judi Dench films her first scenes as M.

February 10, 1995: Q Lab scenes are shot, with Desmond Llewelyn returning once more to the role of gadget master Q.

February 14, 1995: The cast and crew moves to Monte Carlo to shoot the harbour scenes, ultimately postponed due to bad weather.

March 1, 1995: The car chase between the Aston Martin DB5 and the Ferrari F355 is shot in the south of France.

March 14, 1995: Shooting of the chemical weapons facility scenes is held at Leavesden, with Sean Bean on his first day as Alec Trevelyan.

March 21, 1995: The sauna fight between Bond and Xenia is shot.

April 24, 1995: Pierce Brosnan and Joe Don Baker shoot Bond's arrival at St. Petersburg airport, shot on Epsom Racecourse.

May 10, 1995: Shooting of the climactic fight between Bond and Trevelyan on the antenna begins.

June 6, 1995: *GoldenEye* wraps principal photography.

July 1995: The *GoldenEye* teaser trailer makes its debut on the syndicated US television program *Extra*. It was later attached to the prints of Roger Donaldson's movie *Species*.

September 1995: Tina Turner begins recording the main title song for *GoldenEye*, written by Bono and The Edge.

October 19, 1995: The *GoldenEye* novelization by John Gardner is published by Boulevard Books.

October 26, 1995: Tina Turner's "GoldenEye" music video, directed by Jake Scott, is broadcasted on TV for the first time.

October 29, 1995: *The World of 007*, a 45 minute James Bond special hosted by Elizabeth Hurley, is broadcasted on Fox in the United States to promote the imminent release of *GoldenEye*.

November 7, 1995: The single for Tina Turner's "GoldenEye" main title song is released by EMI Parlophone.

November 13, 1995: *GoldenEye* has its world premiere at the Radio City Hall in New York City.

November 14, 1995: The *GoldenEye* soundtrack by Eric Serra is released on CD and cassette by Virgin Records.

November 16, 1995: *GoldenEye* opens in Canada.

November 17, 1995: *GoldenEye* opens in the United States.

November 22, 1995: *GoldenEye* has its Royal Premiere at the Odeon Leicester Square in London.

November 24, 1995: *GoldenEye* opens in the United Kingdom, Ireland and Poland.

December 7, 1995: *GoldenEye* opens in Argentina, Netherlands and Singapore.

December 8, 1995: *GoldenEye* opens in Israel, Portugal and Sweden.

December 10, 1995: *GoldenEye* opens in Slovenia.

December 14, 1995: *GoldenEye* opens in Hungary.

December 15, 1995: *GoldenEye* opens in Brazil, Switzerland, Finland, Iceland, Mexico and Turkey.

December 16, 1995: *GoldenEye* opens in Japan and South Korea.

December 20, 1995: *GoldenEye* opens in Belgium, France and Spain.

December 21, 1995: *GoldenEye* opens in Hong Kong.

December 22, 1995: *GoldenEye* opens in Luxembourg and Malaysia.

December 25, 1995: *GoldenEye* opens in Panama.

December 26, 1995: *GoldenEye* opens in Australia, Norway and New Zealand.

December 28, 1995: *GoldenEye* opens in Germany.

December 29, 1995: *GoldenEye* opens in Austria.

January 4, 1996: *GoldenEye* opens in the Czech Republic, Philippines and Slovakia.

January 12, 1996: *GoldenEye* opens in Greece and Italy.

January 19, 1996: *GoldenEye* opens in Russia.

January 26, 1996: *GoldenEye* opens in Denmark.

February 9, 1996: *GoldenEye* opens in Estonia.

May 21, 1996: *GoldenEye* is released on VHS and Laserdisc.

March 26, 1997: *GoldenEye* is released on DVD in the US, with James Bond debuting in this new home video format.

August 25, 1997: *GoldenEye 007* for Nintendo 64 is released worldwide.

September 24, 1998: *GoldenEye* is first released on DVD in the UK.

September 27, 1998: *GoldenEye* has its US TV premiere on NBC.

December 4, 1998: *GoldenEye* has its TV premiere in Argentina on TELEFE.

January 1, 1999: *GoldenEye* has its TV premiere in Brazil on Globo.

January 2, 1999: *GoldenEye* has its TV premiere in Germany on ZDF, and in Austria on ORF.

March 4, 1999: *GoldenEye* has its TV premiere in Spain on TV3.

March 10, 1999: *GoldenEye* has its UK TV premiere on ITV.

October 19, 1999: *GoldenEye* is released on Special Edition DVD in the US, along with other six James Bond movies.

March 26, 2001: *GoldenEye* is released on Special Edition DVD in the UK.

November 22, 2004: *GoldenEye: Rogue Agent* is released by Electronic Arts for PlayStation 2 and other console platforms.

November 7, 2006: *GoldenEye* is released on a two-disc Ultimate Edition DVD, along with the James Bond catalogue.

November 2, 2010: The Nintendo Wii version of *GoldenEye 007* is released by Activision, as well as another version for Nintendo DS.

November 1, 2011: *GoldenEye 007: Reloaded*, a high-definition version of the *GoldenEye 007* remake for Nintendo Wii, is released for PlayStation 3 and XBOX 360

September 25, 2012: *GoldenEye* is released on Blu-ray, along with the rest of the James Bond catalogue.

SOURCES:
MI6 Confidential magazine (issue 31).
James Bond Wiki (https://jamesbond.fandom.com/wiki/007_franchise_timeline).
The Internet Movie Database (www.imdb.com).

BIBLIOGRAPHY

Books

- Barnes, Alan and Hearn, Marcus. *Kiss Kiss Bang! Bang!* New York: Overlook, 1998
- Bouzereau, Laurent. *The Art of Bond.* New York: Abrams, 2006
- Chapman, James. *Licence To Thrill: A Cultural History of The James Bond Films.* New York: I.B. Tauris, 2007
- Duncan, Paul. *The James Bond Archives.* Colonia: Taschen, 2015
- Fleming, Ian. *Casino Royale.* London: Pan Books, 1955
- Fleming, Ian. *Diamonds Are Forever.* London: Pan Books, 1958
- Fleming, Ian. *Doctor No.* London: Pan Books, 1963
- Fleming, Ian. *From Russia With Love.* London: Pan Books, 1963
- Fleming, Ian. *Goldfinger.* London: Pan Books, 1965
- Fleming, Ian. *Moonraker.* London: Pan Books, 1971
- Fleming, Ian. *You Only Live Twice.* London: Pan Books, 1965
- France, Michael. *GoldenEye.* First draft (January 1994)
- Gardner, John. *For Special Services.* London: Coronet, 1995.
- Gardner John. *Role of Honour.* London: Orion, 2012.
- Gardner, John. *The Man From Barbarossa.* London: Orion, 2012.
- Gardner, John. *GoldenEye.* London: Orion, 2012.
- Johnstone, Iain. *The World Is Not Enough: A Companion.* London: Boxtree, 1999
- Lane, Andrew. *Movie Stunts & Special Effects: A Comprehensive Guide to Planning and Execution.* London: Bloomsbury, 2014.
- Parker, Matthew. *Goldeneye: Where Bond Was Born.* London: Hutchinson, 2014
- Pearce, Garth. *The Making of GoldenEye.* London: Boxtree, 1995
- Pfeiffer, Lee and Lisa, Phillip. *The Incredible World of 007.* New York: Citadel Press, 1995
- Rubin, Steven Jay. *The Complete James Bond Movie Encyclopedia.* Chicago: Contemporary Books, 1995

Magazines and other material

- *007 Magazine*, issue 29, 1996.
- *Cinefantastique*, December 1995.
- *Collecting 007*, issue 16, winter 2000.
- *GoldenEye* Preliminary Production Notes, January 1995.
- *GoldenEye* First Draft, 1994.
- *MI6 Confidential*, issue 31, August 2015.
- *Political Communication*, vol. 22, 2005
- *Starlog*, September 1989.
- *The Official GoldenEye Collector's Magazine*, Illinois: Sendai, 1995.

Web Sites

- 007 Dossier, The (www.the007dossier.com)
- 007HomeVideo.com
- Artistic Licence Renewed (www.literary007.com)
- BibleStudy.org
- Bond Bulletin, The (www.thebondbulletin.com)
- Chicago Tribune (www.chicagotribune.com)
- CNN.com
- CommanderBond.net
- Digital Bits, The (www.thedigitalbits.com)
- Evening Standard (www.standard.co.uk)
- FilmTracks.com
- GameSpot.com
- GoldenEye Dossier, The (goldeneyedossier.blogspot.com)
- IGN.com
- James Bond International Fan Club, The (www.007.info)
- Los Angeles Times (www.latimes.com)
- MI6-HQ.com
- NintendoLife.com
- Russia Beyond ES (es.rbth.com)
- Secret Agent Lair, The (secretagentlair.blogspot.com)
- WinstonChurchill.com
- YouTube.com

Personal correspondence with

- Colclough, Ben
- Last, Kimberly
- Lyons, Derek
- Spaiser, Matt
- Wakeman, Reuben
- Zenhäusern, Yannick

NOTES

[1] Clink, Thomas (2003, April 11). The Royale Treatment: Casino Royale As Literature. *CommanderBond.net*. Retrieved from http://commanderbond.net/1966/the-royale-treatment-casino-royale-as-literature.html

[2] Parker, Matthew. *Goldeneye: Where Bond Was Born*. London: Hutchinson, 2014. Digital, p.32

[3] Biddulph, Edward (2015, August). The Legacy of GoldenEye. *MI6 Confidential*, Issue 31, p. 4

[4] Ian Fleming and Operation Golden Eye: Interview with Mark Simmons (2018, September 25). *Artistic Licence Renewed*. Retrieved from https://literary007.com/2018/09/25/ian-fleming-and-operation-golden-eye-interview-with-mark-simmons/

[5] Parker, *Goldeneye: Where Bond Was Born*, p.26

[6] Licensed to kill with the least thrilling of names (2008, May 27). *Evening Standard*. Retrieved from https://www.standard.co.uk/news/licensed-to-kill-with-the-least-thrilling-of-names-6678043.html

[7] James Bond, 89; Ornithologist's Name Made Famous in Fiction (1989, February 17). *Los Angeles Times*. Retrieved from https://www.latimes.com/archives/la-xpm-1989-02-17-mn-2821-story.html

[8] Fleming, Ian. *Casino Royale*. London: Pan Books, 1955. Print, p. 56.

[9] Fleming, Ian. *Diamonds Are Forever*. London: Pan Books, 1958. Print, p. 150

[10] Fleming, Ian. *Moonraker*. London: Pan Books, 1971. Print, p.157-158.

[11] Fleming, Ian. *You Only Live Twice*. London: Pan Books, 1965. Print, p. 178

[12] GoldenEye - The Road To Production (2003, June 24). *MI6-HQ*. Retrieved from https://www.mi6-hq.com/sections/articles/ge_roadtoproduction

[13] Goldberg, Lee (September, 1989). James Bond's Final Mission? *Starlog*, p.65-66. Retrieved from http://www.the007dossier.com/007dossier/post/2015/05/26/James-Bonds-Final-Mission

[14] Suszczyk, Nicolás (2019, March 28). INTERVIEW: Jeff Kleeman, former United Artists VP, on GoldenEye's success and Bond 25. *The Secret Agent Lair*. Retrieved from http://secretagentlair.blogspot.com/2019/03/interview-jeff-kleeman-former-united.html

[15] Ibid.

[16] Coate, Michael. (2015, November 17). A Post Cold War Era Bond: Remembering "GoldenEye" on Its 20th Anniversary. *The Digital Bits*. Retrieved from http://www.thedigitalbits.com/columns/history-legacy--showmanship/remembering-goldeneye-20th

[17] Duncan, Paul. *The James Bond Archives*. Colonia: Taschen, 2015. Print, p. 427

[18] Jones, Alan (1995, December). GoldenEye: Directing Bond. *Cinefantastique*, p. 23

[19] Fleming, Ian. *Goldfinger*. London: Pan Books, 1965. Print, p. 9

[20] Barnes, Alan and Hearn, Marcus. *Kiss Kiss Bang! Bang!* New York: Overlook, 1998. Print, p. 193

[21] Gardner, John. *Role of Honour*. London: Orion, 2012. Print, p. 18-26

[22] Gardner, John. *For Special Services*. London: Coronet, 1995. Print, p. 215-222

[23] Gardner, John. *The Man From Barbarossa*. London: Orion, 2012. Print, p. 194.
[24] The Lost Art of Interrogation: Starr Parodi & Jeff Fair Interview (2013, December 3). *The GoldenEye Dossier*. Retrieved from https://gedossier007-archived.blogspot.com/2013/12/the-lost-art-of-interrogation-starr.html
[25] Mendelson, Scott (2015, April 8). When 'GoldenEye,' 'Mission: Impossible' Reinvented The Movie Trailer. *Forbes*. Retrieved from https://www.forbes.com/sites/scottmendelson/2015/04/08/when-goldeneye-mission-impossible-reinvented-the-movie-trailer/
[26] Suszczyk, Nicolás (2019, March 28), *The Secret Agent Lair*.
[27] Martin Campbell on the *GoldenEye* Audio Commentary, available on the BluRay edition of the film (20th Century Fox, 2012)
[28] Black, David (2012, May 7). BMW Z3. *The James Bond International Fan Club*. Retrieved from http://www.007.info/bmw-z3/
[29] Chapman, James. *Licence To Thrill: A Cultural History of The James Bond Films*. New York: I.B. Tauris, 2007. Print, p. 74-75; 82.
[30] Ibid., p. 215-216
[31] The Lost Art of Interrogation: Daniel Kleinman Interview (2013, January 25). *The GoldenEye Dossier*. Retrieved from https://gedossier007-archived.blogspot.com/2013/01/the-lost-art-of-interrogation-daniel.html
[32] France, Michael. *GoldenEye*. First draft (January 1994), digital version retrieved from https://www.dailyscript.com/scripts/Goldeneye.pdf
[33] Duncan. *The James Bond Archives*, p. 427
[34] You Can't Do One (2018, April 24). *MI6-HQ*. Retrieved from https://www.mi6-hq.com/sections/articles/timothy-dalton-turned-down-a-third-james-bond-film
[35] Fleming, Ian. *From Russia With Love*. London: Pan Books, 1963. Print, p. 28-29.
[36] Pearce, Garth. *The Making of GoldenEye*. London: Boxtree, 1995. Print, p. 67
[37] Boris Yelstin's real-life Defence Minister during the events of *GoldenEye* was, ironically, a Russian Army General: Pavel Grachev (1948-2012).
[38] Ibid., p. 68
[39] De La Peña Ontanaya, Javier. La traición de los cosacos en la Segunda Guerra Mundial. *Russia Beyond*. Retrieved from https://es.rbth.com/sociedad/2013/01/27/la_traicion_de_los_cosacos_en_la_segunda_guerra_mundial_24275
[40] Chruchill, Winston (1940, June 18). Their Finest Hour. Retrieved from https://winstonchurchill.org/resources/speeches/1940-the-finest-hour/their-finest-hour/
[41] Gardner, John. *GoldenEye*. London: Orion, 2012. Print, p.104-105.
[42] Duncan, *The James Bond Archives*, p. 427
[43] *GoldenEye* Preliminary Production Notes (January 1995), digital version retrieved from https://drive.google.com/file/d/1HJHNprlD1q5N8NtIND4oUEigLLCDbzOo/view
[44] Gardner, *GoldenEye*, p. 113
[45] Ibid., p.154-155.
[46] Ibid., p. 155.
[47] Izabella Scorupco talks about her role in 'GoldenEye', the Bond Girl legacy, and her

career (2004, January 2). *MI6-HQ*. Retrieved from https://mi6-hq.com/news/index.php?itemid=1059
[48] GoldenEye's Girls (2015, August). *MI6 Confidential*, Issue 32, p. 20
[49] Pearce, *The Making of GoldenEye*, p. 66
[50] Gardner, *GoldenEye*, p. 31
[51] Ibid., p. 156
[52] Ibid., p. 95
[53] Ice Ice Baby, *The Official GoldenEye Collector's Magazine*, Illinois: Sendai, 1995. Print, p.21
[54] Johnstone, Iain. *The World Is Not Enough: A Companion*. London: Boxtree, 1999. Print, p. 20
[55] Barnes and Hearn, *Kiss Kiss Bang! Bang!*, p. 195
[56] Ibid., p. 69
[57] Minnie Driver Talks About Her New Thriller 'Spinning Man'. *Today*. Retrieved from https://youtu.be/IKClBB5ZZAk (Video).
[58] Davenport, Caillan (2017, December 31). Who was Janus, the Roman god of beginnings and endings? *The Conversation*. Retrieved from http://theconversation.com/who-was-janus-the-roman-god-of-beginnings-and-endings-86853
[59] The Meaning of Numbers: The Number 6. *BibleStudy.org*. Retrieved from http://www.biblestudy.org/bibleref/meaning-of-numbers-in-bible/6.html
[60] The Meaning of Numbers: The Number 7. *BibleStudy.org*. Retrieved from http://www.biblestudy.org/bibleref/meaning-of-numbers-in-bible/7.html
[61] How the Soviet Union Collapsed: Inside the August Coup d'Etat, *History Channel* documentary, retrieved from https://www.youtube.com/watch?v=jk1Ru35IzdA&t=3s (Spanish version)
[62] Gardner, *GoldenEye*, p.73
[63] Chapman, *Licence To Thrill: A Cultural History of The James Bond Films*, p. 213
[64] Pearce, *The Making of GoldenEye*, p. 124
[65] Ibid., p. 101
[66] Ibid., p. 124
[67] Jones, *Cinefantastique*, p. 22
[68] Pfeiffer, Lee and Lisa, Phillip. *The Incredible World of 007*. New York: Citadel Press, 1995. Print, p.234
[69] Chapman, *Licence To Thrill: A Cultural History of The James Bond Films*, p. 221
[70] Sherman, Matt. An Interview with Don McGregor. *Collecting 007*, Issue 16, Winter 2000, p. 42-43
[71] The GoldenEye Generation - Benjamin Lind (2017, May 14). *The GoldenEye Dossier*. Retrieved from https://gedossier007-archived.blogspot.com/2017/05/the-goldeneye-generation-benjamin-lind.html
[72] The GoldenEye Generation - Austin Skinner (2017, December 16). *The GoldenEye Dossier*. Retrieved from https://gedossier007-archived.blogspot.com/2017/12/the-goldeneye-generation-austin-skinner.html

[73] Gilboa, Eytan. The CNN Effect: The Search for a Communication Theory of International Relations, *Political Communication*, vol. 22:27-44. London: Taylor & Francis Inc, 2005. Digital. Retrieved from http://www.guillaumenicaise.com/wp-content/uploads/2013/10/the-cnn-effect.pdf

[74] Fleming, Ian. *Doctor No*. London: Pan Books, 1963. Print, p. 34

[75] Pearce, *The Making of GoldenEye*, p. 87

[76] Clemmensen, Christian (Rev. 2008, December 9). GoldenEye by Eric Serra. *FilmTracks*. Retrieved from http://www.filmtracks.com/titles/goldeneye.html

[77] Grieve, Drummond (2019, February). DVD Overview. *007 Home Video*. Retrieved from http://www.007homevideo.com/dvd.html

[78] GoldenEye: From the Big Screen to the Small Screen (2016, May 20). *The GoldenEye Dossier*. Retrieved from https://gedossier007-archived.blogspot.com/2016/05/goldeneye-from-big-screen-to-small.html

[79] Bouzereau, Laurent. *The Art of Bond*. New York: Abrams, 2006. Print, p. 14

[80] Lane, Andrew. *Movie Stunts & Special Effects: A Comprehensive Guide to Planning and Execution*. London: Bloomsbury, 2014. Print, p. 127

[81] Big Bangs (2015, August). *MI6 Confidential*, Issue 31, p.14

[82] Duncan, *The James Bond Archives*, p. 443

[83] Ibid.

[84] Chowdhury, Ajay (2015, August). The Man With The Golden Eye. *MI6 Confidential*, Issue 31, p.27

[85] Rye, Graham (1996) Danger - Tank on the Loose! *007 Magazine*, Issue 29, p.32-33

[86] Rubin, Steven Jay. *The Complete James Bond Movie Encyclopedia*. Chicago: Contemporary Books, 1995. Print, p. 478

[87] Classified Information, *The Official GoldenEye Collector's Magazine*, p.51

[88] Ibid.

[89] Bonds Away, *The Official GoldenEye Collector's Magazine*, p.58

[90] Pearce, *The Making of GoldenEye*, p.31

[91] Jones, *Cinefantastique*, p. 23-24

[92] Ibid., p. 24.

[93] Cerulli, Mark (2015, August). Golden Memories. *MI6 Confidential*, Issue 31, p. 32

[94] Pearce, *The Making of GoldenEye*, p. 69

[95] The Legend Lives On (2017, August 25). *MI6-HQ*. Retrieved from https://www.mi6-hq.com/sections/articles/gaming_ge64_legend?id=04303

[96] Hollis, Martin (2006, May 26). The Making of GoldenEye 64. *MI6-HQ*. Retrieved from https://www.mi6-hq.com/sections/articles/gaming_ge64_making_of.php3?id=01180

[97] Perry, Doug (1997, August 25). GoldenEye 007. *IGN*. Retrieved from https://www.ign.com/articles/1997/08/26/goldeneye-007

[98] Gertsmann, Jeff (1997, August 19). GoldenEye 007 Review. *GameSpot*. Retrieved from https://www.gamespot.com/reviews/goldeneye-007-review/1900-2544509/

[99] Fatt, Boba (2007, April 24). The 52 Most Important Video Games of All Time. *GamePro*. Retrieved from https://web.archive.org/web/20100404032903/http://www.gamepro.com/article/features/11

0069/the-52-most-important-video-games-of-all-time-page-5-of-8/
[100] Hollis (2006), *MI6-HQ*.
[101] McFerran, Damien. Exclusive: Martin Hollis Talks GoldenEye 64 Development In This New Interview. *NintendoLife*. Retrieved from http://www.nintendolife.com/news/2016/04/exclusive_martin_hollis_talks_goldeneye_64_development_in_this_new_interview
[102] Gertsmann, Jeff (2004, November 22). GoldenEye: Rogue Agent Review. *GameSpot*. Retrieved from https://www.gamespot.com/reviews/goldeneye-rogue-agent-review/1900-6113810/
[103] Perry, Duglass C. (2004, November 22). GoldenEye: Rogue Agent. *IGN*. Retrieved from https://www.ign.com/articles/2004/11/22/goldeneye-rogue-agent-7
[104] The Lost Art of Interrogation – Grant Kirkhope Interview (2013, March 1). *The GoldenEye Dossier*. Retrieved from https://gedossier007-archived.blogspot.com/2013/03/the-lost-art-of-interrogation-grant.html
[105] Mc Shea, Tom (2010, November 4). GoldenEye 007 (2010). *GameSpot*. Retrieved from https://www.gamespot.com/reviews/goldeneye-007-review/1900-6283589/
[106] Harris, Craig (2010, November 2). GoldenEye 007 Review. *IGN*. Retrieved from https://www.ign.com/articles/2010/11/02/goldeneye-007-review-2
[107] Pearson, Craig (2014, January 1). Ten top fan-remade classics you can play for free right now. *PC Gamer*. Retrieved from https://www.pcgamer.com/ten-top-fan-remade-classics-you-can-play-for-free-right-now/2/
[108] Lind, Benjamin (2018, September 11). Early gameplay footage of 'GoldenEye 25' revealed. *The Bond Bulletin*. Retrieved from https://www.thebondbulletin.com/early-gameplay-footage-of-goldeneye-25-revealed/
[109] Ibid.
[110] Siskel & Ebert At the Movies - GOLDENEYE (1995), retrieved from https://www.youtube.com/watch?v=MYy4PZmvyvA (Video)
[111] Wilmington, Michael (1995, November 17). Saving Bond. *Chicago Tribune*. Retrieved from https://www.chicagotribune.com/news/ct-xpm-1995-11-17-9511170004-story.html
[112] Buckland, Carol (1995, November 21). 'GoldenEye': 007's license to thrill renewed. *CNN*. Retrieved from http://edition.cnn.com/SHOWBIZ/Movies/9511/goldeneye/review.html

Made in the USA
Monee, IL
03 July 2022